Prayers of the Bible

Prayers of the Bible

EQUIPPING WOMEN TO CALL ON GOD IN TRUTH

SUSAN HUNT

PUBLISHING
P.O. BOX 817 • PHILLIPSBURG • NEW JERSEY 08865-0817

Printed in the United States of America

Library of Congress Cataloging-in-Publication Data

Hunt, Susan, 1940-
  Prayers of the Bible : equipping women to call on God in truth / Susan Hunt.
    p. cm.
  Includes bibliographical references (p.   ).
  ISBN 978-1-59638-387-6 (pbk.)
  1. Bible--Prayers--History and criticism. 2. Christian women--Religious life. I. Title.

BS680.P64H86 2011
248.3'209--dc23

2011032269

To the Tuesday Morning Women's Bible Study
at Grace Covenant Presbyterian Church (PCA),
Dallas, Georgia.

These are the women with whom I first shared what I was
learning as we studied the prayers of the Bible together. Their
questions, comments, and prayers taught and inspired me.
They are the coauthors and prayer supporters of this study.

And to the Pastors and Elders of Grace Covenant,
with gratitude for their prayers, encouragement, and oversight
of our women's ministry and of this project.

The LORD *is near to all who call on him,*
to all who call on him in truth.

Psalm 145:18

CONTENTS

INTRODUCTION

How do we approach the magnificent and mysterious topic of prayer? How do we learn to pray?

Our women's Bible study committee had determined that we wanted to study prayer, but then we were faced with these questions. We considered various books and plans but left the meeting without an answer.

I awoke during the night and began praying. Suddenly it was clear. Go to the Bible. Go to the *prayers* in the Bible. Then I slept well.

The next morning I made a list of the prayers that came to mind, and then read them from the perspective that these were the passionate prayers of God's people in the context of daily life and relationships. The more I read, the more excited I became about exploring these prayers with my sisters in Christ.

There are many prayers I could have selected. The rationale for my choices is that my heart was drawn to these specific prayers and to this order—not a chronological order but an order that seems to unfold a pilgrimage of prayer.

PSALM 145

Our Bible study committee selected Psalm 145:18 as our theme verse: "The LORD is near to all who call on him, to all who call on him in truth."

The nearness of God is an extraordinary idea. Little did we realize that this concept captures the essence of every prayer we would study.

When it was decided to publish this study, women committed to pray one day a week. They selected verses from Psalm 145 to shape their prayers.

THE TRUE WOMAN

I am committed to Titus 2 discipleship.[1] In Titus 2, the apostle Paul calls the church to teach God's people sound doctrine. Then he tells Pastor Titus, "Older women . . . are to be reverent . . . and so train the young women . . ." (vv. 3–4). While all discipleship is not gender-specific, there should be some opportunities for women to disciple women to live for God's glory as women. As I thought about applying the topic of prayer to women, I realized that only true women *can* call on God in truth.

More than ten years ago I first encountered the term *the true woman*. I was immediately intrigued and inspired by this nineteenth-century concept of womanhood.

I never found a definitive explanation of what the nineteenth-century church, or women, meant by the term. It seems they assumed everyone understood it. The true woman was often defined by her virtues, but in my opinion she represented more than outward conformity to a moral code. My conclusion was that the true woman was the product of the God-centered theology brought to our shores by our forefathers and foremothers.

In *The True Woman* I wrote,

Some of the Greek words translated true . . . in the New Testament include unconcealed, actual, true to fact . . . the reality at the basis of an appearance. . . . The true woman is the real thing.

She is a genuine, authentic Masterpiece. The Master set eternity
in her heart and is conforming her to His own image. There is
consistency in her outward behavior because it is dictated by
the reality of her inner life. That reality is her redemption.[2]

The true woman is a reflection of redeemed
womanhood.

Whether I'm right or wrong in my conclusions, we know that we
are in a crisis of womanhood. The world's definition of womanhood is the antithesis of God's calling for His daughters. This is
not a call to return to the nineteenth century. It is a call to return
to Scripture. It is a call to true women to call on God in truth.

My Prayer

Writing on prayer has been daunting because I feel inad-
equate. The only reason I dared do so is because God tells us
that He chooses to use the foolish, weak, low, and despised
"so that no human being might boast in the presence of God"
(1 Cor. 1:29). I gratefully admit that "I have uttered what I did
not understand, things too wonderful for me, which I did not
know" (Job 42:3). I pray that you go beyond what I have written
and discover things too wonderful for *us*.

I encourage you to read this study with an open Bible. I
hope you spend more time in the Book than in this book. Read
slowly and meditate on the Scriptures. Whether you study alone
or with others, I encourage you to use the Leader's Guide for
additional thoughts on each prayer.

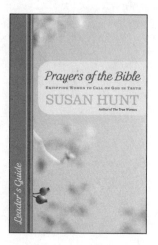

PRAYERS FROM
PSALM 145

When I asked the women in our Bible study to pray Psalm 145 for this project, I had no intention of sharing their prayers with anyone. But I never imagined the power of this endeavor in my own life, in their lives, or in our fellowship as our hearts were united in praying a specific passage of Scripture. I share a few of their prayers with their permission. I think this is appropriate because they were also praying for you.

Monday, Sharon: Psalm 145:13–14

Dear Lord, lift Susan up as she bows before You to write this book. May it be a work that will survive through many generations and lift up the prayer life of all who read it. Give her strength, good health and Your might as she strives toward her deadline.

Tuesday, Dana: Psalm 145:18–20

O Lord, Your word assures us that You will be near to those who call on You in truth. I lift up Your servant Susan to You. May she feel Your nearness each time she sits down to write. Hear her when she cries out to You for help. Rescue her as You have promised. May this book be faithful to Your word.

Wednesday, Denise: Psalm 145:10–13

Give Susan energy, space, and truth so this book will build Your kingdom for this generation and for every generation to come. Through this book, may *all* see Your splendor and glory and goodness. May all see Your truth. May all know You better. Work through our Susan, Lord, so she may show the world, with the precision of Your grace, the splendor and glory and wonder and beauty of eternal, immortal, invisible YOU, King of kings, Lord of lords. Susan is Your workmanship, and I know You will accomplish Your purposes through her. Thank You, Father. Amen. And Amen.

Thursday, Anne: Psalm 145:8–13

Lord, be gracious and merciful to Susan as she writes. May her work bring glory to Your kingdom and tell of Your power, mighty acts and majesty. May this book help spread Your word from generation to generation.

Friday, Tracy (our practical one): Psalm 145:14

Lord, uphold Susan when her vertigo and lack of confidence make her fall, and lift her up when she is tired, discouraged, and has writer's block.

And Elise committed to be the second line of defense and to pray every day for those who were praying: that the Lord will raise up those who are bowed down (v. 14), draw their eyes to look to Him (v. 15), give them faith as they pray, and preserve and keep them (v. 20).

The L*ORD* *is near to all who call on him,*

to all who call on him in truth.

Psalm 145:18

1

REDEEMED

GENESIS 1–3

Biblical womanhood is part of the story of redemption. It can only be understood in the context of this amazing gospel story that begins . . .

BEFORE THE BEGINNING

Read Ephesians 1:1–14

In this marvelous doxology to the triune God, we learn that before creation the Father chose us in Christ (v. 4), that the Son redeemed us through His blood (v. 7), and that the Spirit seals and guarantees our inheritance (v. 13–14). In this covenant of redemption each person of the Trinity assumed a different function in the accomplishment of our redemption, but the common purpose is the praise of His glorious grace (vv. 6, 12, 14). The Bible is the unfolding story of this glorious plan and purpose.

Consider this question: Which Trinitarian function is most important for our salvation?

The answer: The Father, Son, and Holy Spirit are "the same in substance, equal in power and glory,"[1] but each has a distinct, *equally important*, function in our redemption. These functions are so perfectly complementary that they harmonize to accomplish the grand work of redemption that praises God's glorious grace.

THE BEGINNING

Read Genesis 1:1–3

God commanded light to appear. Light did not dare disobey. The authority of God's Word brought creation into existence.

Foundational reality: Our authority
is God's Word.

Read Genesis 1:26

Being created in God's image means that we were created to live in relationship with Him and to reflect certain aspects of His glorious character.

Foundational reality: Our purpose is God's glory.

Read Genesis 1:27

"Male and female"—fascinating—God did not create a genderless being!

By creating the man first, God assigned him the function of headship. The man and woman were created equally in God's image but each was designed for a different, equally valuable function in God's kingdom.

Foundational reality: Gender distinctiveness is God's plan; thus it is very good.

Wayne Grudem explains:

The equality and differences between men and women reflect the equality and differences in the Trinity. . . . In 1 Corinthians 11 Paul writes, "But I want you to understand that the head of every man is Christ, the head of a wife is her husband, and the head of Christ is God (v. 3)." . . .

When did the idea of headship and submission begin? *The idea of headship and submission never began!* It has *always existed* in the eternal nature of God himself. . . .

We can say then that a relationship of authority and submission between equals, with mutual giving of honor, is the most fundamental and most glorious interpersonal relationship in the universe. . . . And when we begin to dislike the very idea of authority and submission—not the distortions and abuses, but *the very idea*—we are tampering with something very deep. We are beginning to dislike God himself.[2]

Read Genesis 1:28

The male and female distinctiveness was so wondrously complementary that together they could glorify God by fulfilling the cultural mandate to be fruitful and multiply and have dominion over God's kingdom.

Read Genesis 2:15–17

God made a covenant of works with the man. Adam was our representative in this covenant. If he and the woman obeyed God perfectly they (and we) would live with God forever. They (and we) would know His nearness. Obedience meant life. Disobedience meant death. It still does.

GOD'S FEMALE DESIGN

Read Genesis 2:18

It was not good for the man to be alone because God created him with the need for a helper. Their interdependence was not weakness; it was the strength and beauty of the relationship. Their interdependence reflected the unity and diversity of the Trinity.

In this verse we are given more insight into God's female design.

Helper is not an inferior function. The Hebrew word translated *helper* in Genesis 2:18 is *ezer*. In the Old Testament it often refers to God as our Helper. Understanding how God is our Helper shows the strong, relational, nurturing, compassionate character of this word. The following are some examples.

- He defends: "The God of my father was my help, and delivered me from the sword of Pharaoh" (Ex. 18:4).
- He sees and cares for suffering: "But you do see, for you note mischief and vexation, that you may take it into your hands; to you the helpless commits himself; you have been the helper of the fatherless" (Ps. 10:14).
- He supports: "May he send you help from the sanctuary and give you support from Zion!" (Ps. 20:2).
- He protects: "Our soul waits for the LORD; he is our help and our shield" (Ps. 33:20).
- He delivers from distress: "But I am poor and needy; hasten to me, O God! You are my help and my deliverer; O LORD, do not delay!" (Ps. 70:5).
- He pities: "For he delivers the needy when he calls, the poor and him who has no helper. He has pity on the weak and the needy, and saves the lives of the needy" (Ps. 72:12–13).
- He comforts: ". . . you, LORD, have helped me and comforted me" (Ps. 86:17).

SIN

Read Genesis 3:1–13

When the man and woman rejected God's authority they lost their relationship with Him; thus they lost their ability to glorify Him. Sin separates us from God. Without His nearness they could not reflect Him. We reflect that which we face, and they turned away from God. They lost their ability to be and do what they were created to be and do.

The woman lost her ability to be a helper.

The true woman became a new woman.

Our first parents were covenant breakers but God is a covenant keeper. Because of the covenant of redemption He did not forsake them. They hid but He came near, not with a sword but with a promise. Neither Satan's deception nor man's disobedience could stop the triune God's covenant loyalty to those on whom He set His affection before creation.

REDEMPTION

Read Genesis 3:14–15

Embedded in the curse on Satan is the first revelation of the gospel. Obedience was still required, so God promised to send One who would obey in our place. This covenant promise thunders through Scripture and through history as God declares, "I will walk among you and will be your God, and you shall be my people" (Lev. 26:12; also see Gen. 17:7; John 1:14; Rev. 21:1–3). This is a covenant of grace. It is not deserved and cannot be earned. It can only be accomplished by the Redeemer who would be the seed of the woman.

Surely Adam was stunned as he listened. The seed of the woman. . . . He and the woman would have children. . . . They deserved death but received life. What was his response to this gospel promise? In celebration and affirmation of his belief in the promise, "The man called his wife's name Eve, because she was the mother of all living" (Gen. 3:20).

Adam named his wife. In Scripture, naming indicates headship. Because of the gospel, Adam was restored to headship.

Eve means "giver of life." This is not just biological. Because of the gospel, she was restored to her ability to be a life-giving helper in every relationship, situation, and season of life. This is our redemptive calling, but our own sin and the influence of culture tempt us to be life-takers—to live for self. Is it really possible for us to fulfill our high and holy calling? Yes, because Jesus said, "I will ask the Father, and he will give you another Helper, to be with you forever, even the Spirit of truth. . . . He dwells with you and will be in you" (John 14:16–17). We can be helpers because, "God is our refuge and strength, a very present help in trouble" (Ps. 46:1).

The true woman knows that her privilege of nearness to God and her ability to call on Him in truth are gifts of His grace. She is awash with gratitude.

How Do We Call on God in Truth?

• With gratitude for our redemption.

Throughout this study we will identify principles that answer this question. This is not an exhaustive answer, and the order is unimportant. I am not suggesting a formula to be followed. These are simply principles based on the Scriptures we will study. The principles are not gender-specific, but we will make application to women by sharing the life-giving prayer stories of some true women.

LIFE-GIVING PRAYER

In his church newsletter, Pastor Glen Knecht wrote about attending a church service in Ukraine after the fall of communism.

How mistaken the Communists were when they allowed the older women to continue worshipping together! It was they who were considered no threat to the new order, but it was they whose prayers and faithfulness over all those barren years held the church together and raised up a generation of men and young people to serve the Lord. Yes, the church we attended was crowded with these older women at the very front, for they had been the stalwart defenders and maintainers of Christ's Gospel, but behind them and alongside them and in the balcony and outside the windows were the fruit of their faithfulness, men, women, young people, and children. We must never underestimate the place and power of our godly women. To them go the laurels in the Church in Ukraine.[3]

Several years after I heard this I was in a church in Ukraine, speaking for a women's conference. I told the story, and my translator looked at me in amazement. "My grandmother was like that," she said. "I was a communist so she never spoke to me about Jesus but somehow I knew. Her home and her marriage were different. Now I am a Christian. I know I am an answer to her prayers." We celebrated. We knew we had heard a life-giving story.

Reflect and Pray

1. Read Ephesians 1:1–14 and write a prayer thanking the triune God for who He is and what He has done for you.
2. Think about the three foundational realities mentioned under the section "The Beginning."
   - How do these foundational realities differ from the cultural perspective of authority?
   - How do they differ from the cultural perspective of our life purpose?
   - What is your reaction to the quote from Wayne Grudem?
3. What is your response to the concept of redeemed womanhood?
   - Reflect on the "helper" verses. What are some ways you have seen women exemplify these characteristics? What are some results when women fail to exemplify these graces?
   - What difference would it make in your relationships if you are a giver of life? A taker of life?
   - Think about your most difficult relationship. Pray about what it would mean to be a giver of life in

that relationship, and ask the Holy Spirit to be your Helper to empower you in fulfilling your calling in that relationship.

- What difference would it make in your prayer life if God's Word was your authority and God's glory was your purpose?

The LORD *is near to all who call on him,*
to all who call on him in truth.

Psalm 145:18

GLORIFY

JOHN 17:1–5

Jesus' high priestly prayer is the pinnacle of calling on the Lord in truth. His nearness with the Father and His love for us are so intensely personal that it almost seems inappropriate to dissect and study this prayer, yet it is recorded for our instruction.

Consider what some fathers of the faith have said about this prayer.

Arthur W. Pink:

> In this wonderful prayer there is a solemnity and elevation of thought, a condensed power of expression, and a comprehensiveness of meaning, which have affected the minds and drawn out the hearts of the most devoted of God's children to a degree that few portions of Scripture have done.[1]

Martin Luther:

> This is truly, beyond measure, a warm and hearty prayer. He opens the depths of his heart, both in reference to us and to

his Father, and He pours them all out. It sounds so honest, so simple; it is so deep, so rich, so wide, no one can fathom it.[2]

James Boice:

> The Scottish Reformer, John Knox, had this prayer read to him every day during his final sickness, and in the closing moments of his life he testified that these verses continued to be a great comfort and a source of strength for his conflict. This prayer should be to us something of what the burning bush was to Moses, for here we hear God speaking, and we should put off our shoes and bow humbly, being about to tread on the most hallowed ground.[3]

OVERVIEW

The prayer divides into three sections:

- vv. 1–5: Christ's prayer for Himself
- vv. 6–19: His prayer for His disciples
- vv. 20–26: His prayer for all believers who would follow

There are five petitions but Jesus tenderly instructs us by giving more than the petitions. He draws us into the grand scope of the redemption story by giving us the *reasons* for the petitions. Each petition is grounded on the glorious doctrines of grace. The work of the triune God in planning, accomplishing, and applying redemption hovers over this remarkable prayer.

The setting is the upper room. This is the last time Jesus will be with His disciples before His betrayal and crucifixion. The emotion and urgency of His words are palpable.

Read John 16:33—17:1

Jesus had been looking at His disciples and speaking to *them*; then His focus changes. He looks to His Father and speaks to *Him* about *them*. The term *Father* shows the intimacy of the relationship.

> From preaching He passed to prayer! Thereby He teaches us that after we have done all we can to promote the holiness and comfort of those with whom we are connected, we should in prayer and supplication beseech him, who is the author of all good, to bless the objects of our care and the means which we have employed for their welfare.[4]

The more intimately a true woman knows her heavenly Father, the more often she will shift her focus to Him and commit people and situations to his sovereign care.

Read John 17:1 and 5

In this first petition, Jesus prays that the Father will *glorify* Him and that He will *glorify* the Father.

To understand this prayer, as well as other prayers we will study, we must know the biblical meaning of *glory*, and yet we are often fuzzy in our understanding of this concept. Part of the difficulty is that even if we find a definition, it does not always fit the passage. Sometimes it seems that contradictory things are said about Christ's glory. In this passage Jesus asks God to *restore the glory* that He had before creation, and yet in John 1:14

31

the disciple wrote: "We have *seen his glory.*" How could they see it if He didn't have it?

The explanation is that there are two aspects of God's glory— internal and external.

His *internal glory* refers to His attributes.

> God's glory consists of his intrinsic worth, or character, to use a human term. Thus, all that can be properly known of God is an expression of his glory. . . . When the disciples beheld his glory . . . they actually beheld his character, which was the character of God.[5]

This is the glory Jesus retained while on earth. He showed us the character of God.

His *external glory* refers to visible manifestations.

> In Jewish thought any outward manifestation of God's presence was believed to involve a display of light, radiance, or glory so brilliant that no man could approach it. . . . Light was also associated with the cloud of glory that overshadowed the wilderness tabernacle during the years of Israel's wandering and that later filled Solomon's great temple in Jerusalem (1 Kings 8:10–11).[6]

Before the incarnation Jesus possessed internal and external glory, but He laid aside the external manifestation of His glory when He came to earth. Here He asks for it to be restored.

Read John 17:2

Jesus gives the reason for this petition: Redemption hinges on this request.

The Father had given the Son universal *authority* in order that the Son could give *eternal life to all whom [the Father had] given Him.* God gave Him universal authority (see Matt. 28:18), but the purpose is specific. Charles Spurgeon pastors our souls in his explanation of this transcendent wonder:

> It is in virtue of this [universal] power that the gospel is preached to all men. . . . I can preach a gospel which, in its proclamation, is as wide as the ruin and as extensive as the fall. . . . The text tells us that the object and design of all this was not universal, but special . . . that the chosen may receive life—that the elect may be filled with spiritual life on earth, and afterwards enter into the glory-life above. . . . My text seems to me to present that double aspect which so many people either cannot or will not see. Here is the great atonement by which the Mediator has the whole world put under his dominion; but still here is a special object for this atonement, the ingathering, or rather outgathering of a chosen and peculiar people unto eternal life.[7]

"All whom you have given [me]" refers to the covenant of redemption entered into prior to creation by the Father, Son, and Holy Spirit. Jesus' prayer is shaped by God's eternal plan and purpose.

As Jesus approaches the cross, He is consumed with the specific people God had given Him. If you trust Jesus for your salvation you are one of those gifts the Father gave the Son; you were on His heart and mind in this prayer of our living Savior just before His death.

His petition to be glorified is not self-centered; it is God-centered and sinner-centered. Jesus asks to be glorified so that the Father will be glorified and sinners will be justified.

Unless Christ is glorified—unless He is raised from the dead and ascends to glory—the work of redemption will not be accomplished.

Two themes emerge: God's glory and God's people. We will see these themes in other prayers we study.

Read John 17:3

Jesus clearly and concisely explains that eternal life is *knowing God*—simple words that convey a profound mystery.

Knowing God is more than having intellectual information; it is nearness.

Before the beginning of time, the transcendent God planned for immanence. Distance is contrary to His nature. The triune God covenanted to choose, redeem, and indwell a people so they could know Him and display His glorious grace before heaven and earth "not only in this age but also in the one to come" (Eph. 1:21).

Jesus said, "I know my own and my own know me, just as the Father knows me and I know the Father" (John 10:14–15).

He knows His own because they have belonged to Him since eternity past. He laid aside the brilliant manifestation of His glory to come and live in nearness to them. He came to claim them so they could live in nearness to Him both now and forever.

Knowing God is a relationship with Him through Jesus. It is a relationship initiated by God. It is a relationship that transforms us from life-takers to life-givers.

Here we see a third theme: God's nearness.

Read John 17:4

How did Christ glorify the Father while He was on earth? He accomplished His work made in the covenant of redemption. This anticipates His cry from the cross, "It is finished" (John 19:30).

Our work—our calling—is to glorify God in all of life. We glorify Him by reflecting His character in every relationship and situation.

> The true woman knows that her calling to glorify God is costly. It means dying to self so that the life of Christ may fill her and overflow from her.

The words of James Boice instruct and challenge us:

The divine pattern is first self-denial, obedience, and suffering, after which the glory follows. This should be our pattern also. We must seek to glorify Christ while we live by showing forth his character. But this will not happen in some mystical way. It will happen only as, by the grace of God, we walk in his will (as He directs), as we carry out whatever responsibility He has entrusted to us, as we point to Jesus as the only way of salvation, as we finish our work, and as we seek the glory of God in its fullness, rather than our own.[8]

The fourth theme is God's calling.

How Do We Call on God in Truth?
- Pray for His glory.
- Pray according to His eternal plan and purpose.

Life-giving Prayer

In 1967, Joni Eareckson Tada was paralyzed in a diving accident. Although she battles intense pain, she travels the world ministering to others. In 2010 she was diagnosed with breast cancer. The following are excerpts from an article by Susan Olasky in *World* magazine.

> I started with a question about her daily routine, and she said, "Let's pray, because that's how I always start."
>
> She tells me that she's recovering from pneumonia and has limited lung capacity, something that's particularly dangerous for a quadriplegic. She does breathing exercises, and when I ask what that means she breaks into a hymn: "Breathe on me, Breath of God, fill me with life anew, that I may love what thou dost love, and do what thou wouldst do."
>
> "Hymn singing," she says, "Reminds me to fix my mind on Jesus" so as not to "grow weary and lose heart."
>
> She sees herself in a battle against "powers and principalities that want us to despair" and emotions that "take me down dark, grim paths." . . . The battle requires her active participation. She takes as a theme Hebrews 10:38: "But my righteous one shall live by faith, and if he shrinks back, my soul has no pleasure in him." Her voice is emphatic: "I do not want to be one of those who shrink back. I don't want to tarnish his name. . . . God's up to something big. How can I showcase him to others?"
>
> She knows her life is on display and that others are watching and learning by her response: "I am on this battlefield. How can I glorify God?"[9]

Reflect and Pray

1. What preceded this prayer? Read John 13–16.
2. What followed this prayer? Read John 18–19.

3. Read John 17. How many times does Jesus refer to the ones the Father gave Him?

4. Read the following and write a summary of what you learn from them about knowing God.

   Jeremiah 24:7
   John 10:14
   Ephesians 1:17
   Philippians 3:10
   2 Timothy 2:19
   1 John 2:3–6; 3:24; 5:13, 18–20

5. What difference will it make in your prayers if you intentionally ask God: How can I glorify You in this situation/relationship?

The LORD is near to all who call on him,
to all who call on him in truth.
Psalm 145:18

SANCTIFY

JOHN 17:6–19

The heartbeat of this prayer is for our spiritual needs. This is not to say that Jesus is unconcerned about our physical needs, but His foremost concern is for our foremost need. The two petitions in this section, as well as the two in the next section, rest on His first request, that He be glorified. His victory over sin and death and His triumphal ascension secure His petitions for us.

The disciples listened as Jesus prayed for them. We must listen too; He was praying for us.

Read John 17:6

Jesus tells us four things about those for whom He prays:

1. They are God's. God owns everything by right of creation, but this verse refers to possession by redemption.

2. God gave them to Jesus. We are His by divine fiat. We did nothing to deserve or earn this favored status.

3. Jesus made God's name known to them. God's name refers to His attributes, words, and deeds. He reveals Himself through various names. The name that Jesus revealed in a unique way is *Father*. He taught the disciples to pray, "Our Father," showing us the intimacy of the relationship. James Boice explains:

> It is true that in one sense the word "Father" for God is as old as religion. Even the Greeks spoke of "Father Zeus." . . . But in this case the word really means "Lord." In Israel God was also said to be the Father of His people [Isa. 64:8; Ps. 103:13]. . . . But this is characteristically of the people as a whole; nowhere, either in the Old Testament or in any other document prior to the time of Jesus, does any individual Israelite ever address God directly as "my Father."[1]

4. They kept God's Word. The Greek word means to pay attention to or observe. The point is not that they obeyed perfectly but that they submitted to the authority of God's Word.

Read John 17:7–8

Jesus gives another sequence of four to explain the process by which we become His disciples.

1. Jesus gave the disciples the words God gave Him.
2. The disciples received the words.

3. On the basis of those words they came to know that Jesus came from God.
4. They believed that God sent Jesus.

The believer is one who has been given God's Word—words of life that accomplish God's purpose in us.

Jesus was not naïve about the faith and fortitude of the disciples, but He knew the power of God's Word. He knows that spiritually we are shamefully sluggish, but He also knows that His Word is in us and that the Word will produce gospel fruit.

Read John 17:9–10

Jesus again underscores the identity of the ones He pleads for—the ones claimed by the Father, given to the Son, and empowered by the Spirit to reflect His glory.

Read John 17:11–12

Jesus was leaving but they were staying, so in this petition He prays that God will keep them. What a comforting concept. The psalmist rejoiced that "The LORD is your keeper. . . . The LORD will keep you from all evil. . . . The LORD will keep your going out and your coming in from this time forth and forevermore" (Ps. 121:5,7–8).

Jesus' use of the title *Holy* Father is significant. The One who is our Father is the majestic, glorious King who said, "For I am the LORD your God. . . . Be holy, for I am holy" (Lev. 11:44).

His holiness is a reminder of our most dangerous threat—our sin! It is sin that distances us from God. Growing in holiness keeps us near, but we have no power *in* ourselves to *keep* ourselves *from* ourselves. The resource He provides is the power of His name.

We have twelve grandchildren. As I studied this petition and contemplated the fierce temptations faced by young people, I began fervently praying that God will keep them. But the more I pondered and prayed the more I realized that this request also means praying that they will pursue holiness. I began asking God to keep them by giving them a deep hatred for their own sin and the sin of the world and by giving them a heart that is quick to repent when they do sin.

I love Proverbs 18:10 and say it often to our grandchildren: "The name of the LORD is a strong tower; the righteous man runs into it and is safe."

Running into Him means running away from sin. "Holy Father, may they run hard in both directions."

Judas is not mentioned in Jesus' prayer as an exception. "The case of Judas does not teach that a born-again person can be lost. But it does teach what would inevitably happen if God did not regenerate the individual and then keep in his care the one who has been so regenerated. If it were not for God, who could stand? Who could survive the onslaughts of the world if God did not keep us."[2]

Read John 17:13

At first glance it seems as if Jesus interrupts His petition, but this is no interruption; this is the reason for the petition.

He *speaks these things*—He states His requests and reasons *out loud*. This is not the first time the disciples heard Him speak about joy. Before He prayed He talked to them:

> If you keep my commandments, you will abide in my love, just as I have kept my Father's commandments and abide in his love. These things I have spoken to you, that my joy may be in you, and that your joy may be full. (John 15:10–11)

He knows us well. He knows that we are often not joyful. We are sinners and we live in a fallen world. We are easily defeated and discouraged. We look for happiness in all the wrong places. Neither our situation nor our personality will give us joy. We cannot manufacture joy. Jesus wants us to have *His* joy, and He wants us to know that He has made complete provision for it to be so, even though we are faced with sin within and sin without.

Read John 17:14–16

He continues the petition by moving from His joy in us to the world's hatred for us. The world hates us because God's Word is in us. We need not only to be kept from our own sin, but to be protected from the evil one. The resource He has given us is His Word.

Read John 17:17

D. Martyn Lloyd-Jones explains that this petition "is, of course, intimately connected with, and is, in a sense, a continuation of the first. His great desire is that his people should be kept by God. . . . How then are they to be kept? And the answer is that they are to be kept by being sanctified."[3]

The Westminster Shorter Catechism defines sanctification as "the work of God's free grace, whereby we are renewed in the whole man after the image of God, and are enabled more and more to die unto sin, and live unto righteousness."[4]

Sanctification is a lifelong process. John the Baptist captured its essence: "He must increase, but I must decrease" (John 3:30).

The means by which such a marvel takes place is God's Word, which is truth. "This implies that God's Word does not simply conform to some other external standard of 'truth,' but that it is truth itself; that is, it embodies truth and it therefore is the standard of truth against which everything else must be tested and compared."[5]

The prayer of Psalm 119 is another favorite that I pray for myself and our grandchildren and recite to them:

> Turn my heart toward your statutes
>   and not toward selfish gain.
> Turn my eyes away from worthless things;
>   preserve my life according to your word. (Ps. 119:36–37, NIV)

The true woman intentionally seeks to measure every decision by the standard of God's Word and to submit every relationship and circumstance to the authority of his Word.

Read John 17:18–19

Jesus was sent on a mission, and so are we. Jesus was sent to glorify the Father by saving sinners. We are sent to glorify the Father by proclaiming the glories of His grace in word and deed. This is the work He has given us to do. We represent Him in the world.

Jesus gives us more than our mission; He gives us His merit. Don't miss the wonder of His words, "I consecrate myself." He was not conscripted. He voluntarily set Himself apart as our Redeemer, Substitute, Sacrifice, Mediator, and Intercessor so that we can be sanctified. His finished work is the authority by which we fulfill our calling.

Read John 17:6–19 again

Two threads run through verses 6–19: the power of His name and the power of His Word. Jesus knew that His time had come to return to heaven. He knew the weakness of the men He had entrusted with the gospel. He knows my weakness. But overriding it all He knows the power of the Word that has been implanted in us, and He knows the power of His name.

His Word bids us approach the Father in prayer, and it is by Jesus' name that we do so.

> Whatever you ask in my name, this I will do, that the Father may be glorified in the Son. If you ask me anything in my name, I will do it. (John 14:13–14)

Praying in Jesus' name means asking for what is consistent with His Word and asking on the basis of His merit.

How Do We Call on God in Truth?

- Approach Him as our Father.
- Pray in Jesus' name.
- Pray according to His Word.

As Arthur Pink says:

The Word of God is "quick and powerful" (Heb. 4:12), not only in its effects on us, but also in its moving power with God himself. If this were more realized by Christians, the very language of Holy Writ would have a larger place in their supplications, and more answers from above would be obtained. . . . How can we more honour him in our prayers than by employing the very words of Scripture, his words, rather than our own?[26]

LIFE-GIVING PRAYER

James Boice tells a wonderful story.

All of us have scenes from childhood that we remember gratefully. . . . I think back on them with growing thanksgiving as the years go by. Some of the scenes I remember thankfully are when my mother would gather our family together to read Psalm 121 and pray with us before one of the children left home or the family started on a trip.

He will not let your foot slip—
    he who watches over you will not slumber . . .
The LORD will keep you from all harm—
    He will watch over your life;
the LORD will watch over your coming and going
    Both now and forevermore.

I can close my eyes and see our family seated in a circle in our living room and hear those words now. This was my mother's psalm for her family. Because so many of those "goings out" and "comings in" were my own, there is a sense in which Psalm 121 became my travel psalm.[7]

Reflect and Pray

1. Read John 17:6–19 several times and write a prayer based on this passage.
2. What are your thoughts about the privilege of calling the King of kings "Father"?
3. Reflect on Psalm 119:36–37. What are some of the worthless, selfish things you need to ask God to turn you from? Compare these with the Worthy One to whom we turn.
4. Look at the "helper" verses in chapter one. Remember that Jesus consecrated Himself so you might become a life-giver, and that He has provided all the resources you need.

The LORD *is near to all who call on him,*
to all who call on him in truth.

Psalm 145:18

4

UNIFY

JOHN 17:20–26

The triune God has known me from all eternity; I have known Him for almost fifty years. This morning, after reading and meditating on this extraordinary prayer, I wrote the following in my prayer journal:

> I am overcome with gratitude that I am privileged to call You Father and increasingly aware that Jesus won this privilege for me because You gave me to Him in eternity past. The longer I know You the more I see this truth of Your love with childlike wonder. Father, keep this gratitude and wonder ever-growing, never dimming.

In a matter of hours Jesus will suffer the horror of the crucifixion, but He talks to His Father about us. The theme that was whispered in previous portions of this prayer explodes in this section: love. This juxtaposition of the cross and love is overwhelmingly incompatible with our fallenness; yet it is perfectly in sync with His nature. For God so loved that He gave; when we love, we take. Jesus came to show and tell a new way of love.

Read John 17:20

Now He looks beyond the disciples to all His elect ones who will follow until He returns. He sees before Him the company of the redeemed both past and present. We are all bundled together in His love. The people and the petitions are magnificently interrelated. His glorification assures us that He is powerful enough to keep and sanctify us. His covenant love for those the Father gave Him assures us that He will do so. The Lover of our souls now pushes His petitions heavenward with a longing that is staggering.

Read John 17:21–22

Here we peer into one of the great mysteries of Scripture: union.

The perfect unity of the Trinity is a mystery we cannot fathom. Equally astounding is that we are drawn into this union, through redemption sovereignly planned, purchased, and applied. This is the promise of God's covenant, that "I will dwell among you," and it is the theme of His nearness.

Throughout the New Testament we read the phrases "in Christ," "in Jesus," and "in Him" that show our oneness with our Savior. This union is called a mystery because we cannot fully understand it, but we can ponder it and praise the God who loves us so much.

In this petition Jesus prays that our union with Him will overflow in unity with one another. The means He has provided for this human impossibility in His glory. He deposits in us His glory—His character—so we can reflect Him to each other. As we show His love, grace, mercy, and forgiveness to each other, our hearts will be bound together in a unity that will stand as a witness to the world.

This unity is far more profound than organizational unity. Spurgeon explains it as "a unity of persons who have received, not common life as all have, but life eternal . . . brought into vital union with the person of the Lord Jesus . . . persons to whom God's name has been manifested; people who have seen what others never saw."[1]

This is Jesus' prayer for His church, the covenant community, His family. We are one because of our adoption in Christ. Our positional unity is a gift of grace. Our privilege and our responsibility are to nurture this unity in practical ways so that our local churches are vibrant witnesses to the gospel.

Read John 17:23

This prayer pulsates with Jesus' covenant love for us, but here is perhaps His most extraordinary revelation: The Father loves us even as He loves Jesus.

It would be beyond arrogance for us to say or even think such a thing, but it's true. Boice explains:

God's love for us is in the same measure and is exercised in the same way as his love for Christ. There have been attempts to avoid this meaning, no doubt because it is so tremendous . . . but they miss the full force of the sentence because they do not take the key word at full value. That word is *kathos*, which means "just as" or "to the same degree that." Thus, we are told that God loves those who are Christ's to the same degree and in the same way that he loves Christ.[2]

How do we know that He loves us as He loves Christ? The Bible tells us so: "God shows his love for us in that while we were still sinners, Christ died for us" (Rom. 5:8).

Read John 17:24

Here is the final petition: He wants us with Him so we can see His glory.

Weren't the disciples right there with Him? Yes, but He was looking beyond the cross to His Father's home, where His external glory would be restored. Jesus was so transported to where He would be that it was as though He was already there.

This is what praying according to His Word will do. It propels us upward to the heavenlies. What will be becomes more real to us than what is.

Who does Jesus want to be with Him where He is going? Again, we see the covenantal theme: those whom the Father gave Him.

> I feel right glad that there is no sort of personal character mentioned here, but only—"those whom Thou hast given Me." It seems as if the Lord in His last moments was not so much looking at the fruit of grace as at grace itself; he did not so much note either the perfections or the imperfections of His people, but only the fact that they were His by the eternal gift of the Father.[3]

Here we have fellowship in His sufferings (Phil. 3:8–11). There we will have fellowship in the fullness of His glory.

In this concluding statement, Jesus focuses on what is immediately ahead. When we pray according to His Word, we focus on heavenly realities. This fortifies us to face earthly realities. The heavenly minded are equipped to do earthly good.

He says He will continue to make God's name known so that God's love can be in us. How will He "continue to make it known"? By completing what He came to do. The God of Glory, nailed to a tree to redeem those the Father gave Him before creation, is an unparalleled demonstration of love. This completed work of love empowers His people to love; we can love sacrificially only through Christ dwelling in us.

The Greek word used here for love is *agape*. This word is not simply a warm feeling of emotion. It is a new thing planted in us by the Holy Spirit. Love that gives rather than takes is the fruit of the Spirit. We do not have this ability to love apart from Christ in us. This love has the capacity to grow.

> The true woman passionately pursues love by pursuing Christ. She prays that she might decrease so that love might increase.

Thus Jesus ends where He began, with love. When the disciples gathered in the upper room:

> Jesus knew that his hour had come to depart out of this world to the Father, having loved his own who were in the world, he loved them to the end. . . . He laid aside his outer garments,

and taking a towel, tied it around his waist. Then he poured water into a basin and began to wash the disciples' feet. . . . When he had washed their feet and put on his outer garments and resumed his place, he said to them, "Do you understand what I have done to you? . . . If I then, your Lord and Teacher, have washed your feet, you also ought to wash one another's feet. For I have given you an example, that you also should do just as I have done to you." (John 13:1,4–5,12,14–15)

There may be no greater way for us to "wash the feet" of our brothers and sisters than to faithfully pray for God to be glorified in them, to ask Him to keep and sanctify them, to pursue profound unity with them, and to anticipate spending eternity praising God's glorious grace with them. Remember that our High Priest offered this prayer in the hearing of His disciples; He continues to pray it in the presence of His Father.

How Do We Call on God in Truth?
• With an eternal perspective, seeing ourselves united in love to Christ and to the great company of the redeemed from all ages.

LIFE-GIVING PRAYER

Sharon Betters' sixteen-year-old son Mark was killed in an automobile accident in 1993. I am grateful to my friend for the treasure of her encouragement[4] in sharing with me God's ministry to her in this excruciating experience.

After Mark's death, the Bible looked like black marks on a page but I knew my only hope was to soak in the Word. Every morning I wrote a prayer that described with brutal honesty how I felt, then I read the Proverbs and Psalms with the same date (February 1: Proverbs 1 and Psalm 1). I asked God to show me one truth and then I expanded on it in my journal. These journals are a record of how God personally came into that room with me and slowly led me back to himself. At the beginning of this grief journey my prayers were more of a lament for myself and for my husband and children than a proclamation of God's grace.

About two years after Mark's death, God led me to read the book of John in order to get to know him better. I stayed in John 17 for an extended time because it read like an intimate journal entry written by Jesus himself. I personalized it by inserting my name each time Jesus referred to "those You gave me" or "who will believe in me." This is an emotional passage for me because it was truth speaking to my emotions and felt like a love letter from God. Jesus thought about me in one of the most horrific moments of his life. His love for his church forced me to consider how I could love the church even in my grief. Slowly my prayers expanded to include others. This was a choice I made out of obedience because emotionally I had little energy to carry anyone else's burdens. Yet, it is another way God strengthened me. Jesus' prayer encouraged me to keep making choices to cultivate community when I had no desire to do so.

Not always, but many times, God gave me "treasures in the darkness" from Scriptures that coincided with the very prayers I had written in my journal before reading.

Reflect and Pray

1. Read verses 20–26 several times.
   - What are some practical ways others have helped you feel united to your church family?
   - How are you challenged to nurture unity in your relationships with other Christians?

2. Read the "one anothering" verses below and think about specific ways to put these into action.
   - Romans 12:9–13
   - Romans 15:1–7
   - Hebrews 10:24–25
   - 1 Peter 4:9
   - 1 John 3:11, 16–18

3. What difference would it make in your life and prayers if you took time to reflect on the eternal perspective of your union with Christ and with other Christians?

The LORD *is near to all who call on him,*
to all who call on him in truth.

Psalm 145:18

5

NEARNESS

Exodus 32−34

E xodus is an epic adventure about the deliverance of the Israelites from slavery, but the real blockbuster is the *purpose* of the book: the continuing drama of redemption. This narrative is about God keeping the promise to bring those He gave to Jesus near to Himself.

God's nearness to His people is a double struggle that is both cosmic and personal.

- The first struggle is with the world to let them go.
- The second is in the heart of the redeemed to turn from idols and submit to God's rule.

Exodus gives an extraordinary picture of both struggles.

THE BACKGROUND

In Genesis 12 God sovereignly initiates a relationship with Abram, telling him that the promised seed (Gen. 3:15) will come from his family. We are included in this story: "If you are Christ's, then you are Abraham's offspring, heirs according to promise" (Gal. 3:29).

The picture of the church emerges in Exodus. Abraham's descendants are slaves in Egypt, as God had told Abraham they would be (Gen. 15:13–14). A son is born. He becomes a prince. The hero is humbled; then he is ready (Exodus 2). While shepherding in a desert he sees a visible manifestation of God's glory. He stands on holy ground and receives a holy calling (Exodus 3). In his classic work *Promise and Deliverance* S. G. DeGraff explains:

> The calling of Moses was not initially a call to lead Israel out of Egypt. Moses was to be a mediator between God and the people, so that the Lord could meet the people through him. The Lord had dealt with the patriarchal family through the patriarch himself or through one of the members of his family. Now that there was a covenant people, someone would have to serve as head of that people. This development is a clear foreshadowing of the Christ.[1]

We must have a mediator to draw near.

THE FIRST STRUGGLE: LET MY PEOPLE GO

Exodus 5–12 recounts God's battle to claim His people. The struggle culminates with the sacrifice of the Passover lamb. Blood was shed for the people's deliverance.

In Exodus 19–24 the covenant is established with Israel as a nation. The people ratify the covenant with a bold promise: "All the people answered with one voice and said, 'All the words that the LORD has spoken *we will* do'" (Ex. 24:3).

The arrogance of their self-confidence is preposterous; the second struggle has begun.

Read Exodus 32

It is hard to imagine a more striking contrast than the people's audacious promise in Exodus 24:3 and their quick lapse into idolatry. In this struggle for the heart we are our own worst enemies. We, and those for whom we pray, are prone to idolatry. We declare our obedience but are quickly distracted by boredom, desires, and circumstances, and in our hearts we turn back to the ways of Egypt.

> This [Moses] is the one who was in the congregation in the wilderness with the angel who spoke to him at Mount Sinai, and with our fathers. He received living oracles to give to us. Our fathers refused to obey him, but thrust him aside, and in their hearts they turned to Egypt, saying to Aaron, "Make for us gods who will go before us." (Acts 7:38–40)

> Nevertheless, with most of them God was not pleased, for they were overthrown in the wilderness. Now these things took place as examples for us, that we might not desire evil as they did. Do not be idolaters as some of them were. . . . Therefore, my beloved, flee from idolatry. (1 Cor. 10:5–7, 14)

God said to Moses:

> [Your people] have turned aside quickly out of the way that I commanded them. . . . It is a stiff-necked people. Now therefore

let me alone, that my wrath may burn hot against them and I may consume them, in order that I may make a great nation of you. (Ex. 32:7–9)

It is astonishing that Moses did not agree to this idea but identified with the rebels and prayed for them, foreshadowing the One who became like one of us and passionately prays for God to keep us, sanctify us, unify us, and eventually take us to glory.

Interspersed in the narrative are six petitions. The similarities between Moses' petitions and John 17 remind us of our Intercessor's struggle for us, and teach us about interceding for others.

The First Petition: Remember your promise (Ex. 32:13)

Moses cannot plead for the rebellious people on the basis of their performance, so he pleads on the basis of God's Word.

The Second Petition: Forgive their sin (Ex. 32:32)

His identification with the people is heart-wrenching. "If you will forgive their sin—but if not, please blot me out of your book that you have written" (v. 32). We see this anguished love in Paul: "I have great sorrow. . . . For I could wish that I myself were accursed and cut off from Christ for the sake of my brothers, my kinsmen according to the flesh" (Rom. 9:2). We hear it in the pleading of John Knox, "Give me Scotland or I die." This cry has gone up from the hearts of countless mothers who intercede for rebellious children. But we cannot take the place of another. We cannot be a substitute because we need a Substitute whose identification with His people effected full forgiveness for them. Those for whom we intercede need Jesus.

Read Exodus 33 and 34

The narrative moves forward to confront the crucial question: Will God come near or will He remain at a distance? God tells Moses to take the people to the Promised Land, but that He will not go *among* them. Moses does not budge; he knows that the land without the presence of God would be nothing but a piece of real estate. Jesus pushed His prayer heavenward until He exclaimed, "I want them to be with me!" Moses pushed too.

The Third Petition: Show me your ways that I may know you (Ex. 33:13–14)

Moses prays for the intimacy of knowing God, but he does not pray only for himself. This intercessor's heart cries out, "Consider too that this nation is your people." The response: "My presence will go with *you*, and I will give *you* rest."

What more could Moses desire than God's presence with him? The intercessor wanted God's presence with *them*.

The Fourth Petition: Your presence with us (Ex. 33:15–17)

God's presence is the only thing that will transform stiffnecked people into a community that reflects His glory. Their distinctiveness before the world is never to be about the splendor of wealth. It is about "I in them and you in me, that they may become perfectly one, so that the world may know that you sent me and loved them even as you loved me" (John 17:23). So Moses boldly reaches for still more.

The Fifth Petition: Show me your glory (Ex. 33:18)

Moses had seen the burning bush, the pillar of cloud, and the spectacle at Sinai. What more glory did he expect to see? Was Moses surprised by God's response that He would show Moses the glory of His goodness and His name? But first, God tells him to stand on the rock; then God put him *in* a cleft of the rock. The Rock is Christ (1 Cor. 10:4). Arthur Pink explains:

> In order for sinful man to be able clearly to contemplate the Divine perfections of an infinitely righteous, holy God, it is necessary that he should be put into a place of security and peace. This God *has*, in His infinite condescension and grace, provided for us. To faith that "rock" is Christ. Augustus Top-lady beautifully represented this in his well-known hymn,
>
> "Rock of Ages cleft for me, Let me hide myself in Thee."
>
> Or, as we prefer to sing it,
>
> "Rock of Ages cleft for me, Grace hath hid me safe in Thee."[2]

God answers Moses' prayer:

> The Lord passed before him and proclaimed, "The LORD, the LORD, a God merciful and gracious, slow to anger, and

64

abounding in steadfast love and faithfulness, keeping steadfast love for thousands, forgiving iniquity and transgression and sin." (Ex. 34:6–7)

God reveals Himself as Yahweh, His personal name whereby He binds Himself to His people in covenant loyalty. This name points to Jesus, because it is through Him that we can have a relationship with God.

The attributes God reveals are repeated throughout the Old Testament and form the foundation for appeals to God in prayer and for Hebrew piety. God proclaims His covenant love and mercy to His people despite their sin. This is what Moses needed to know. He knew he could not depend on the people to keep the covenant, and that the only way he could continue to live with and lead stiff-necked people was to gaze at the glorious goodness of God and reflect that glory to them. This was his calling, and ours.

Moses worshiped, and then made his daring final request.

The Sixth Petition: Take us for your inheritance (Ex. 34:9)

Moses does not ask God to *give* the people an inheritance. He asks God to *take them as His inheritance.* The very idea makes us gasp, yet this is the gospel.

A truly marvelous concept . . . one to which our poor minds are quite incapable of rising—that the great and self-sufficient God should deem himself enriched by worms of the earth whom he hath saved by his grace. This "inheritance," like all others, has come in through death, the death of God's own Son. That death not only vindicated Divine justice by putting away the sins of his people, but it has brought in that which shall glorify God through the endless ages of eternity. God will occupy his "inheritance" forever. "Behold, the tabernacle of God is with men, and He will dwell with them, and they shall be his people, and God himself shall be with them, and be their God." (Rev. 21:3)[3]

COVENANT RENEWAL

God said: "Behold, I am making a covenant. . . . And all the people among whom you are shall see the work of the LORD, for it is an awesome thing that *I will do with you*" (Ex. 34:10).

We can't win the struggle in our hearts in our own strength, but because Jesus won the battle over sin and death for us *He* will do an awesome thing with us. *He* will drive out "the Amorites, the Canaanites, the Hittites" (v. 11)—the enemies and idols of our souls. We are justified by grace and we are sanctified by grace.

"When Moses came down from Mount Sinai, with the two tablets of the testimony in his hand . . . Moses did not know that the skin of his face shone because he had been talking with God" (v. 29). Glory visibly radiated from Moses and he didn't know it; the only way we reflect glory is to be unaware of self. This is the awesome thing God does with His inheritance. We do not simply determine to *act* merciful, gracious, loving, and forgiving; this is what we *become*.

The true woman "with unveiled face, beholding the glory of the Lord, [is] being transformed into the same image from one degree of glory to another" (2 Cor. 3:18).

How Do We Call on God in Truth?
• Appeal on the basis of His character.

LIFE-GIVING PRAYER

Elise told me that while shopping she saw a woman from her neighborhood who greeted her and said, "I've been praying for you and your husband." Elise was surprised since she did not know the woman well. The woman explained, "When I walk each morning I pray for my neighbors. Recently I have particularly prayed for your marriage." Elise thanked her. "The Lord is answering your prayers. Our marriage is growing in grace." They chatted about Elise's children, and Elise shared her desire for them to love and serve the Savior. The next day she found a stack of index cards the woman had left at her door. The woman had personalized prayers from Scripture for the children. Here are two examples:

> Keep Emma, Lily and Ethan from all harm. Watch over their life; watch over their coming and going, both now and forevermore. Psalm 121:7–8

> Lead Emma, Lily and Ethan not into temptation, but deliver them from the evil one. Matthew 6:13

"I'm overwhelmed that a woman I do not know well invests so much in our family. I feel protected by her prayers."

One neighborhood . . . one young family . . . one praying woman . . . and only the Lord knows the profound impact of her prayers in their lives, and how those prayers will trickle down through generations.

Reflect and Pray

1. Think about the themes and petitions in John 17. Read Exodus 32–34 again and reflect on the similarities.

2. What are some idols Christian women face?
3. List the attributes of God revealed in Exodus 34:6–7. Compare them with the "helper" verses in chapter one and the fruit of the Spirit in Galatians 5:22. Pray that God will produce this gospel fruit in you.
4. What do you learn about being an intercessor from the account of Moses?

The LORD *is near to all who call on him,*

to all who call on him in truth.

Psalm 145:18

6

FORGIVEN

PSALM 51

David's prayer in Psalm 51 is the next stop on our prayer pilgrimage. It is a prayer of repentance and faith. This is not the prayer of a new pilgrim. David knew the Lord intimately, but the progressing pilgrim goes from "show me your glory" (Exodus 33) to seeing the greatness of her sin. This is the testimony of a forgiven child.

This prayer shows us the way back to nearness, but it is not simply a prayer to have in reserve in the event we get caught in grievous sin. *Every* sin is grievous. We need this psalm every day. It shows us how to *stay* near.

THE CONTEXT

Read 2 Samuel 11:1–12:15

How could he? Who of us has not asked this question when we read of David's adultery and murder? But when I dare look

71

into the depths of my heart I know exactly how he could do this. He was a sinner; so am I. There is no sin that I am not capable of committing.

It seems that David chose leisure in the palace rather than responsibility on the battlefield. Perhaps boredom sent him to the roof. There was nothing inherently wrong with walking on the roof, but when he *saw*, he *inquired*. A seemingly innocent question was one step into darkness. The second step was easier.

David was a covenant-breaker, but he was a covenant-breaker whom the Father had given to the Son, and the triune God is a covenant-keeper. David's authority became his own feelings; his purpose became his own pleasure. But because of God's commitment to keep and sanctify this straying child, God sent Nathan who, with laser precision, identified the core problem: "Why have you despised the word of the LORD?" (v. 12:9).

> The foundational issues are always the same:
> authority and purpose.

> The way back is always the same:
> repentance and faith.

REPENTANCE AND FAITH

Conversion consists of repentance and faith. The Westminster Shorter Catechism explains these graces:

Q. 86: What is faith in Jesus Christ?

A. Faith in Jesus Christ is a saving grace, whereby we receive and rest upon him alone for salvation, as he is offered to us in the gospel.

Q. 87: What is repentance unto life?

A. Repentance unto life is a saving grace, whereby a sinner, out of a true sense of his sin, and apprehension of the mercy of God in Christ, doth, with grief and hatred of his sin, turn from it unto God, with full purpose of, and endeavor after, new obedience.

The first of Martin Luther's Ninety-Five Theses is: "When our Lord and Master, Jesus Christ, said 'Repent,' he called for the entire life of believers to be one of repentance."

Repentance and faith are gifts from God that usher us into His presence, and they are ongoing graces that keep us near.

THE BASIS OF THE APPEAL

Read Psalm 51:1–2

There is no warm-up, no rationalizing, no blame-shifting. David goes straight to God's Word and bases his plea for forgiveness on God's character. The words David uses—mercy, steadfast love, transgressions, iniquity, sin—are the same Hebrew words God spoke to Moses: "The LORD, the LORD, a God merciful and gracious, slow to anger, and abounding in steadfast love and faithfulness, keeping steadfast love for thousands, forgiving iniquity and transgression and sin" (Ex. 34:6–7). David humbly acknowledges the contrast between God's character and his own.

Iniquity means to twist or distort.

> All sin of every sort is deviation from a standard to which we ought to be conformed. . . . If a line be absolutely straight . . . the smallest deflection . . . will run out into an ever-widening distance from the straight line. There is nothing which it is more difficult to get into men's belief than the sinfulness of little sins.[1]

Transgression means to rebel.

> The very centre of all sin is the shaking off of obedience to God. Living to "self" is the inmost essence of every act of evil, and may be as virulently active in the smallest trifle as in the most awful crime.[2]

Sin means to miss the mark.

> Every sin misses the goal at which we should aim. . . . By it we fall short of the loftiest purpose. Whatever we gain we lose more.[3]

THE HEART OF THE BROKEN

Read Psalm 51:3–5

"I know my transgressions" is an agonizing confession but a convincing evidence of grace. While David lived the lie, his heart was so deceived that he was blind to his sin. Now he sees. "If we say we have no sin, we deceive ourselves and the truth is not in us" (1 John 1:8). Sin deceives us; truth exposes us. Brokenness is a gift of grace.

"Against you, you only have I sinned." Of course David had sinned against Bathsheba, Uriah, and the nation, but it was sin because there is a God whose Word is the authority for right and wrong, and because the ones David misused and abused were made in God's image.

"Behold, I was brought forth in iniquity." Not only had David committed sin, he was a sinner. The problem was not external; it was internal. He knew he would continue to sin unless God did a radical work of grace in his heart so, by faith, he boldly believed in the power of the gospel to sanctify a sinner. Isaac Watts' hymn "Joy to the World" captures the idea: "No more let sins and sorrows grow. . . . He comes to make his blessings flow far as the curse is found." No sin is beyond the reach of grace.

THE FUTURE OF THE FORGIVEN

Read Psalm 51:6–12

Note the Trinitarian shape of the future David envisions. He asks God for the ministry of the Son and the Spirit in his broken heart.

Verse 6. He does not want to continue the lie. He wants truth to penetrate beyond his behavior to the core of his being. This points to Jesus, who is truth and wisdom.

Verse 7. To purge means to cleanse from impurities. Hyssop is a plant that was used at the Passover as a brush to put blood on the doorposts of the Israelites' homes so the angel of death would pass over the house (Ex. 12:22), and in ceremonial cleansing to sprinkle blood on one who was unclean (Lev. 14:4, 6; Num. 19:18). We are cleansed and purified by the blood of Jesus.

Verse 8. David acknowledges that God is the one who broke his bones. *Broken*, in the Hebrew, is a strong word that refers to physical and emotional crushing. The bones are the supporting framework of the body. God mercifully crushes every support we depend on to hold us up. Crushing leads to conforming: "For those whom he foreknew he also predestined to be conformed to the image of his Son" (Rom. 8:29). Crushing empties us of self and presses us to Jesus, who prayed that *His* joy would be fulfilled in us (John 17:13). We cannot be full of His joy until we are empty of self.

> As long as sin still lives inside of us, producing in each of us a propensity to forget and wander, God's grace will come to us in uncomfortable forms. You may be wondering where the grace of God is in your life, when actually you're getting it. But it's not the grace of release or relief; no, you're getting the uncomfortable grace of rescue, relationship, and refinement.[4]

Verse 9. Our debt is blotted out because Jesus paid it.

Verse 10. Create is the Hebrew word *bara*, which is used in Genesis 1 and means to create out of nothing. "By employing the term *create*, he expresses his persuasion that nothing less than a miracle could effect his reformation, and emphatically declares that repentance is the gift of God."[5]

Verse 11. "David is not talking about eternal security or the fear of losing his salvation. He is only acknowledging that he is unable to live a holy life without God. Therefore, he needs the help and power of the Holy Spirit every single moment if he is to be able to overcome temptation and seek after godliness."[6]

Verse 12. David did not ask that his salvation be restored. He asked for the joy of restored fellowship. He asked for nearness. Pride has been dealt a crushing blow; David readily admits that he will not even have a willing spirit to stay near unless God upholds him.

A true woman prays for grace to see her sin, to be a quick repenter, and, by faith, to anticipate the blessings of forgiveness.

THE MINISTRY OF THE FORGIVEN

Read Psalm 51:13–17

When we truly repent, we are prone to become stuck in sorrow over our sin and to wallow in guilt. Faith moves on.

When God's mercy touches our misery it becomes a ministry. Sin is never private, it always hurts others. Our restoration can bless others.

> David is reminding us that what qualifies us to teach in the personal ministry context of daily life is the grace that we have received in our own moments of need. This teaching isn't about laying out a comprehensive theology of grace. . . . No, what it's actually about is realizing that my story of God having rescued me by his grace is a tool that God intends to use in the lives of others. . . . So, are you a good steward of your story of grace?[7]

THE HEART OF THE FORGIVEN

Read Psalm 51:18–19

The heart of the forgiven reflects Jesus' heart. Jesus loves His church.

Zion is a hill in Jerusalem that David captured from the Jebusites (2 Sam. 5:7). Eventually the temple was built on this hill and it became known as Mount Zion. It was the place that represented the nearness of God to His people. It often refers to the covenant community and even to the city of God in the new age.

David loves Zion and prays for God to build her up. He concludes by speaking of sacrifices. The sacrifice of Jesus empowers us to "present our bodies as a living sacrifice, holy and acceptable to God, which is your spiritual worship" (Romans 12:1).

David had been meticulous in hiding his sinful actions. Now he opens his heart before God and the church for all ages. Why would he do such a thing? He was forgiven. God's glory and God's people were his consuming passion.

How Do We Call on God in Truth?

• With a repentant and believing heart.

LIFE-GIVING PRAYER

I had spoken on the topic of redeemed womanhood, and a woman lingered behind. "I have been married twenty-five years and have been a life-taker the entire time. Deep down I knew it, but hearing the description of a life-taker and a life-giver forced me to admit it. This is the legacy I have given my children. Is it too late? What can I do?"

I asked if Christ lived in her; she said He did. "Then you have God's Spirit in you. It is never too late." As we talked she realized that the problem was not distance from her husband; it was distance from God. "Spend time in the Word and prayer. Ask the Holy Spirit to give you grace to see specific sins and to repent. Pray that He will transform you into a life-giver in your heart and then in your words and actions."

"I did not want to come to this conference," she confided. "But I couldn't stay away. It has been hard. I've been confronted with my sin, but I have not felt condemned."

"That's grace," I replied. "Jesus paid for your sin. He took the condemnation. He has confronted you in order to transform you. Anticipate what He will do."

Reflect and Pray

1. Meditate on Psalm 51 for several days.
   - Ask God to shine the light of His Truth into your inward being and to show you specific sins that you may be hiding from yourself.
   - Ask Him to show you any supporting structures other than Him that you are trusting.
   - Reflect on the words of the hymn *Joy to the World*.
   - Write your prayer of repentance and faith.

The LORD *is near to all who call on him,*
to all who call on him in truth.

Psalm 145:18

7

FORGIVING

Note the progression of our prayer pilgrimage: We were enfolded in the loving prayer of our Savior, then we prayed with Moses, "Show me your glory," and the sight of His glorious goodness caused us to see our shameful sinfulness. Brokenness, repentance, and faith continually transform us from "one degree of glory to another" (2 Cor. 3:18) until the forgiven ones become the forgiving ones.

God told Moses that "all the people among whom you are shall see the work of the LORD, for it is an awesome thing that I will do with you" (Ex. 34:10). Transforming us into forgivers may be the most awesome thing God does with His people.

HOW MANY TIMES DO I FORGIVE?

Read Matthew 18:21–35

In answer to Peter's question, Jesus told a story that shattered Peter's assumptions about forgiveness. Jesus redefined the topic. Joe Novenson wrote:

> Jesus defines kingdom forgiveness as voluntary incursion of loss of that which is owed to release another from obligated payment. This is the distinctive of kingdom forgiveness in opposition to the world's forgiveness.
>
> A Christian incurs personal loss for the good of another, knowing that Christ did so for us on the cross. Unfortunately words like "I can't forgive until they make it right" are common among those outside and even inside the church. Forgiveness neither demands justice for trespass nor avoids sacrifice for the violator. . . .
>
> Consider afresh the voluntary loss incurred by our covenant-keeping king for his own people. Nothing else will melt the unforgiving, debt-demanding heart and begin to reconcile sinners in Jesus' church.[1]

Jesus concludes the story with a penetrating statement: "So also my heavenly Father will do to every one of you, if you do not forgive your brother from your heart" (verse 35). We cannot fake it; forgiveness must be from the heart. He is never satisfied with mere behavioral conformity because, as David says, "You delight in truth in the inward being, and you teach me wisdom in the secret heart" (Ps. 51:6). Whether it is a crushing violation such as abuse or abandonment, or an insensitive remark by a husband or friend, forgiven ones are to forgive. It is at the cross that we become forgivers.

Prayers from the Cross

A hush falls over my heart as I read these prayers. We cannot and should not equate our situation with Jesus', but there is a progression in His prayers that is instructive for us. Listen with reverence and awe.

Read Matthew 26:36–42

"My soul is very sorrowful. . . . My Father, if it be possible, let this cup pass from me; nevertheless, not as I will, but as you will" (Matt. 26:38–39).

Jesus' submission to the Father's will is foundational. "During the days of Jesus' life on earth, he offered up prayers and petitions with fervent cries and tears to the one who could save him from death, and he was heard because of his reverent submission" (Hebrews 5:7 NIV).

Prayer didn't change the eternal will of God, but it strengthened Jesus to obey God's will and drink the cup. The cup refers to God's wrath (Isa. 51:17), and as Jesus hung on the cross He drank it all. If one drop of God's wrath had passed through His outstretched arms and fallen on us it would have obliterated us. The magnitude of His love compels us to bow to His authority and to live for His glory. This is essential to becoming a forgiver.

Read Matthew 27:46

The agony of Jesus' cry, "My God, my God, why have you forsaken me?" jolts us to remember that the Father turned His face away from the Son because Jesus was covered in *our* sin. He

85

experienced all the pain and horror of separation from God—the full force of hell—so that the ones the Father gave Him will never be separated from God.

We may *feel* abandoned, but we must go to the Word and believe truth and not our feelings. The truth is: "I will be your God, you will be my people, I will dwell among you. I will never leave you or forsake you."

Read Luke 23:34

The suffering of the cross is a shameful cosmic scandal. Suffering usually causes us to become increasingly self-absorbed. We forget everything and everyone but the pain. But in the midst of the pain Jesus asks the Father to forgive those who are inflicting the pain—not simply the soldiers who drove the nails into His flesh, but the ones whose sin drove Him to the cross.

Jesus submitted to the Father's eternal plan and purpose, He suffered hell in order to accomplish that purpose, and He prayed for the forgiveness of those whose sin He bore. The power of this forgiveness frees us from bondage to sin and bursts into our lives to redeem all the effects of the curse of sin. Forgiveness liberates us to forgive. This is, indeed, an awesome thing that God does with His people.

Come now to another time and place and see this awesome power of the cross in a man named Stephen.

Read Acts 6:1–14

Stephen was the recipient of sovereign grace. He was one the Father gave the Son. We know this because he was *full* of the Spirit, wisdom, grace and, power. To be full of one thing, we have to be empty of other things. It is the gospel that empties us of self and fills us with Christ. Emptying involves ongoing repentance and faith and results in the fullness of forgiveness.

Read Acts 6:15

Stephen had yielded to God's authority and embraced God's purpose for him. The evidence is "his face was like the face of an angel." Like Moses, his countenance was transformed because his character had been transformed by the glory of God's goodness. There was no panic, only the peace of one who looks to Jesus in the midst of hostility.

Read Acts 7:1–53

Stephen knew God's Word. He brilliantly recounted the plan and purpose of redemptive history. The religious leaders knew the facts but they did not see that it all pointed to Jesus. I think that when he said, "You stiff-necked people," using the same language God used to refer to their forefathers, he did so with tears.

Read Acts 7:54–60

Stephen's eyes were not on the rage of the crowd. In the power of the Holy Spirit he looked up and saw the glory of God. "I see . . . the Son of Man standing at the right hand of God," he exclaimed.

When Jesus was arrested, the high priest asked Him whether He was the Son of God. Jesus answered, " 'You have said so. But I tell you, from now on you will see the Son of Man seated at the right hand of Power and coming on the clouds of heaven.' Then the high priest tore his robes and said, 'He has uttered blasphemy' " (Matt. 26:64–65). The religious leaders knew that by this title Jesus claimed to be God (see Dan. 7:13–14), and by using this title Stephen acknowledged Him to be so.

Stephen saw the risen Jesus standing to acknowledge him: "Everyone who acknowledges me before men, I also will acknowledge before my Father who is in heaven" (Matt. 10:32). He saw Jesus standing to welcome him. "That's one you gave me. He is a forgiven one because I died in his place." Stephen entrusted himself to Jesus: "Lord Jesus, receive my spirit." Then he looked at his enemies with mercy: "Lord, do not hold this sin against them." The screams and the stones could not silence the prayer of the forgiven one; he repeated the prayer his Savior had prayed for him.

Jesus prayed in John 17 that Stephen would be sanctified by the truth, and Stephen was. He gave Stephen His glory and Stephen reflected the goodness of that glory. He said, "I want him to be where I am and to see my glory," and that prayer was answered.

Our flesh may not be pierced with stones, but our hearts are. We need to rush to the cross, hear the prayers of Jesus, and ponder the price He paid to cancel our debt. We need to look up and see Him waiting for us. We see Jesus in His Word. By His Word and His Spirit we are reminded that we have been forgiven, and we are empowered to forgive.

Forgiveness is a life-giving grace. "See to it that no one fails to obtain the grace of God; that no 'root of bitterness' springs up and causes trouble, and by it many become defiled" (Heb. 12:15).

> The true woman prays for grace to forgive. She knows that unforgiveness defiles many but that forgiveness blesses many.

As Stephen was stoned, Saul watched. Stephen's forgiveness blessed Saul even though Saul did not realize it at the time. Saul became the apostle Paul. Stephen and Paul were not reconciled in this life, although we can only imagine the joy of that reconciliation in heaven. The point: forgiveness does not guarantee reconciliation. The person who stoned your heart may not want reconciliation. He may be dead. But you are to forgive from your heart, and you can because you are a forgiven one and the Spirit of God lives in you.

The master who canceled the servant's debt in Jesus' parable said to the unforgiving servant: "You wicked servant! I forgave you all that debt because you pleaded with me. And should not you have had mercy on your fellow servant, as I had mercy on you?" (Matt. 18:32).

How do we call on God in truth?
• With mercy for those who hurt us.

LIFE-GIVING PRAYER

I asked my friend, one of the most radiantly joyous Christians I know, to share her thoughts about prayer and forgiveness. She asked to remain anonymous because her mother is still alive and she does not want to dishonor her.

> Forgiveness . . . That's something prayer is especially good for. Back in the 80s I was in an Incest Survivors Anonymous group. We were told to pray for people we were having a hard time forgiving. We were instructed to pray that the person would receive all the things that we wanted for ourselves. That didn't sound quite right to me, so I modified it just a bit. I started praying for my "enemies" to receive all the things that Scripture tells us God wants for us to have. That removed me from the equation which seemed (and still seems) like a good idea to me. That's how I was able to forgive my mother and father and the other people who abused me as a child. I found that it was impossible to pray for someone and still hold a grudge against them. When you pray for them, you develop a completely different relationship with them, even if you're never going to see them again.

When I marveled at God's grace in her she said, "I never give it much thought anymore because it all seems to have happened to someone else, it's so long ago. But that, too, is a manifestation of God's grace in forgiveness. I'm not the same broken person I was when I originally needed to forgive. Thanks to God's grace, I'm someone else entirely."

Reflect and Pray

1. What was helpful to you in this chapter?

2. Reflect on the quote from Joe Novenson. What are some losses people may incur when they forgive?

3. Reflect on Hebrews 12:15. Have you seen examples of a woman's bitterness defiling others? Have you seen examples of forgiveness blessing others?

4. Ask the Lord to search your heart and show you whether there is lingering bitterness.

5. What is your reaction to the Life-giving Prayer story?

- Give it to the LORD
- Repent/Confess sin
- Best for others

The LORD is near to all who call on him,
to all who call on him in truth.

Psalm 145:18

8

HELP

2 Chronicles 20

This David-and-Goliath-caliber story could be told alone without context, but that would radically diminish its reach and relevance. Seeing it in the context of the unfolding story of redemption unlocks profound lessons on the privilege, practice, and power of prayer.

The Continuing Story

After the Israelites settled in the Promised Land, God chose David to be king. David wanted to build a house for the Lord to replace the tabernacle, but God said:

> "Moreover, the Lord declares to you that the Lord will make you a house. When your days are fulfilled and you lie down with your fathers, I will raise up your offspring after you, who shall come from your body, and I will establish his kingdom. He shall build a house for my name, and I will establish the throne of his kingdom forever." (2 Sam. 7:11–13)

This Davidic covenant points to Solomon who would build the temple, and ultimately to the Messiah who is the Temple.

At the dedication of the temple Solomon prayed.

Read 2 Chronicles 6:1–7:3; 7:11–16

Even Solomon was astonished at the notion of a house for the name of the Lord. "Will God indeed dwell with man on the earth?" he asked (2 Chron. 6:18). God's nearness is the wonder of the ages.

Everything about the temple showed the way of access to God, and it all pointed to Jesus, who is our access. When Jesus completed the work of redemption, the curtain to the Holy of Holies—the place in the temple where God met annually with man represented by the high priest—was dramatically ripped apart (Luke 23:44–45), so that we can "with confidence draw near to the throne of grace, that we may receive mercy and find grace to help in time of need" (Heb. 4:16).

King Jehoshaphat reached into the remarkable prayer promises made to Solomon and found grace to help in his time of need.

Our secret resource is prayer. And what makes it so important is that the weakest Christian can at any period of his life at any moment of the day and in any circumstance cry out to God for help and instantly have the resources of the infinite, sovereign God at his disposal.[1]

JEHOSHAPHAT'S PRAYER

Read 2 Chronicles 20:1–2

What great multitude is coming against you? Whether it is a health or financial crisis, memories of rejection that flood your mind, a temptation such as emotional lust or bitterness, fear because the enemy is having his way with your teenager, an important decision . . . whatever it is, Jehoshaphat's response to his crisis is a tutorial on the sanctifying power of calling on God in truth.

Read 2 Chronicles 20:3–4

Jehoshaphat's first instinct was not to devise a war plan. He followed the plan already set forth in God's Word: Seek the Lord. In David's charge to Solomon he had said: "If you seek him, he will be found by you" (1 Chron. 28:9). God told Solomon: "If my people who are called by my name humble themselves, and pray and seek my face and turn from their wicked ways, then I will hear from heaven and will forgive their sin and heal their land" (2 Chron. 7:14). If this is not the most astounding prayer promise in Scripture, surely it is on the short list.

The true woman establishes the holy habit of daily seeking the Lord in His Word. When a crisis comes, she does what is her habit to do.

Read 2 Chronicles 20:5–7

Jehoshaphat prayed according to God's eternal plan and purpose. He stood in the temple, acknowledging God's promise and presence. He used the name Yahweh and referred to our fathers, recognizing God's covenant faithfulness to His people. This energized Jehoshaphat to remember God's sovereign power. Spurgeon said, "If we begin by doubting, our prayer will limp."[2]

Read 2 Chronicles 20:8–9

He called on God's name, believing the promise made to Solomon:

> Now my eyes will be open and my ears attentive to the prayer that is made in this place. For now I have chosen and consecrated this house that my name may be there forever. My eyes and my heart will be there for all time. (2 Chron. 7:15–16)

This is another jaw-dropping promise. God's eyes and heart will always be at the temple where He has placed His name. Jesus is our temple (John 2:18–21)—and after His death, resurrection, and ascension He calls *us* His temple, individually and collectively as His church (1 Cor. 3:16; 6:19).

Then Jehoshaphat made his petition.

Read 2 Chronicles 20:10–12

The king's appeal for God to execute judgment on his enemies is based on God's promise to give His people the land. He prays for Israel's protection so that God's name will not be dishonored. He prays for God's glory.

He does not bring a battle plan to God and ask God to bless it. He approaches God empty-handed. "For we are powerless against this great horde that is coming against us. We do not know what to do, but our eyes are on you" is my default prayer. For years I assumed that when there was a problem—whether mine or someone else's—I should have a solution. There was a huge leap in my sanctification when I finally got it—admitted that I'm ignorant and helpless, and trusted God.

Jehoshaphat's humble trust illustrates Proverbs 3:5–6:

> Trust in the Lord with all your heart,
>   and do not lean on your own understanding.
> In all your ways acknowledge him,
>   and he will make straight your paths.

I think the key to this kind of trust is found in Jehoshaphat's name. Stanley Gale explains:

> Jehoshaphat means, "the Lord has judged." . . . Jehoshaphat . . . was not able to face the foe. He was not the deliverer. Jesus, the ultimate Jehoshaphat, was able. He is the God who judges and God incarnate who was judged as he stood in the place of sinners. He is the One, the only one, able to deliver from the definitive crisis. It is in Christ and him crucified that God has judged, the wrath of his justice fully spent, and the guilt of sin atoned for.[3]

The Judge took my judgment. When I trust Him with my eternal soul, I can trust Him with my earthly problems.

Here we see the depth of the Hebrews' trust. The enemy moved closer but they did not panic; they listened to God's Word. Prayer is a conversation. Too often we make it a monologue. We need to be still and listen by reading God's Word and asking the Holy Spirit to give us grace and wisdom.

The massive army approaching was nothing compared with the massive promises they received. They were not given specific details, but the one detail they needed: "The Lord will be with you." The instruction to go forward and face the enemy only makes sense to people who believe this promise and who know the faithfulness and power of the One who promised.

It is noteworthy that they stood together, including the children. The church at prayer is a beautiful sight. When we unite our hearts in prayer we are an answer to Jesus' prayer that we "become perfectly one" (John 17:22–23). We want to protect our children from every crisis, and there are certainly some things they do not need to know, but let's not rob them of experiencing the power of trusting prayer when an enemy is coming against us.

They bowed in worship before they were delivered, because they were delivered from the greatest enemy—fear.

No song is so sweet, methinks, in the ear of God as the song of a man who blesses him for "grace he has not tasted yet"—for what he has not got, but what he is sure will come. The praise of gratitude for the past is sweet, but that praise is sweeter which adores God for the future in full confidence that it shall be well.[4]

Read 2 Chronicles 20:20

They trusted and they obeyed. Prayer does not mean passivity. The work of prayer is active. We seek, praise, petition, and listen, and then move forward trusting God to make our paths straight. He will open doors and He will close doors. Jehoshaphat encourages his people's obedience by reminding them of God's presence and promises. We need to do this for each other.

Read 2 Chronicles 20:21

I love this! Can you imagine the reconnaissance report of enemy spies? "Those fools have put their musicians rather than their tanks at the front!"

A life lived in line with the gospel is just as bizarre to a watching world because the gospel is foolishness to those who are perishing, but it is the power of God to the saved (1 Cor. 1:18).

They went forward singing: "Give thanks to the Lord, for his steadfast love endures forever."

This ancient doxology commemorated God's revelation of His steadfast love to Moses (Ex. 34:6–7). It was sung by David when the ark was returned to Jerusalem (1 Chron. 16:34) and by the singers when Solomon had the ark carried to the Holy

Place in the temple (2 Chron. 5:13). It is a marvelous song that is often repeated in the Psalms and continues to strengthen God's people as we move forward in faith.

Read 2 Chronicles 20:22–26

The people gathered treasures they did nothing to earn. This is the experience of grace. It is the consequence of trusting prayer.

Baracah in Hebrew means "blessing." The wilderness battlefield became a place of blessing. I'm glad they took time to gather the precious things. Too often we rush away from the crisis. We don't want to think about it. But when we take time to ask ourselves questions, we discover great wealth. What did I learn about God? How did He strengthen me for each day? How did He change my heart through this experience? Journaling during a time of crisis helps us to capture the treasure of God's nearness and the unexpected blessings of His grace.

Read 2 Chronicles 20:27–30

What a delightful conclusion. The people of Judah celebrated. They were a witness to the nations. There was quiet and rest. And all because God's people did what He tells us to do—seek help from Him. Isaiah 30:15 describes Jehoshaphat: "For thus said the Lord God, the Holy One of Israel '. . . In quietness and in trust shall be your strength.'"

Quietness refers to our hearts, not our speech. "It implies the absence of strife, war, or trouble on the one hand, and worry or anxiety on the other. . . . This state of peace and tranquility is clearly seen to be dependent on, and a direct result of, God's blessing on an obedient people."[5]

Trust "expresses that sense of well-being and security which results from having something or someone in whom to place confidence. . . . The cause for hope is not in one's merit with God . . . but only because of God's . . . unswerving loyalty, his gracious kindness."[6]

Quietness and trust grow in the heart of one who seeks the Lord.

Jehoshaphat got it right this time, but that was not always the case. This stunning story is sandwiched between two incidents when Jehoshaphat did not seek the Lord (2 Chronicles 18 and 20:36–37). The results were disastrous. Prayer has consequences; so does failure to pray. This story stands as a monument to the blessing of calling on God in truth.

How Do We Call on God in Truth?

• In quietness and in trust.

LIFE-GIVING PRAYER

Patsy Kuipers was thirty-eight when her husband died suddenly of a heart attack. Their daughters were seven and ten. Patsy learned to seek God's will about everything, and she learned to seek the counsel of church leaders and other Christian friends. Her heart became quiet.

Patsy's daughters finished college and married godly young men. Then another "great multitude" came against her. She had been employed by the same company for thirty years. She loved her work, but she began to feel that she didn't belong there anymore. She prayed for grace to be a life-giver in the stressful situation and for wisdom to know God's will about whether to stay or leave. She took a week off and used the time to pray, study God's Word, and journal. Then she asked some friends to pray. She writes:

> In the weeks leading up to my annual review, God gently prepared me by allowing me to read and hear things that gave me assurance and peace. One Sunday our pastor concluded his sermon with these words: "God tells us, I am God, I am in control, I have a plan, I love you." I clung to these truths and when I heard the words, "Your position has been eliminated" I did not panic. My first thought was, "I'm unemployed!" but my second thought came immediately, "Thank you Father for a clear answer. I know you have another plan for me and I did not have the courage to make this decision." I do not know the plan yet but I do know that God is in control and He will guide me each step of the way.

Reflect and Pray

1. What are your thoughts about Jehoshaphat's response to his crisis in 2 Chronicles 20 compared with 2 Chronicles 18 and 20:36–37?
2. What is most helpful to you about 2 Chronicles 20?
3. Reflect on 2 Chronicles 7:14–16. Personalize the passage by writing it in your own words and inserting your name.

The LORD is near to all who call on him,
to all who call on him in truth.

Psalm 145:18

9

KNOWLEDGE

Ephesians 1:15–23

Life often feels jumbled. The pieces don't seem to fit. A family faces the sorrow of a death within hours of the celebration of a birth. Situations and decisions do not come in an orderly fashion—they pile on top of each other. Adult children stray from the Lord and make devastating decisions. A husband walks out on a wife and children. Ephesians 1 is my go-to passage when I hear myself thinking: This isn't fair. This doesn't make sense. She didn't deserve this.

Paul's magnificent doxology to the Trinity realigns my unbiblical thinking. It celebrates God's sovereignty and brilliantly answers the question: If God is sovereign, why pray? James Boice explains:

> If God is in charge of everything and has "foreordained whatsoever comes to pass"—in the words of the *Westminster Shorter Catechism*—what is the point of praying? . . . The reasonable answer to this objection is that although God does do as he pleases, he uses means like prayer, witnessing, Bible reading, and the doing of good works. . . . The first chapter

of Ephesians teaches this lesson clearly. It would be hard to find a passage of Scripture that stresses the sovereignty of God in salvation more strongly (except perhaps Romans 8). Yet it also emphasizes the importance and urgency of prayer just as strongly. Indeed, those two themes give the chapter its shape. . . . For Paul, the knowledge that God was working was an inducement to prayer, not an excuse for neglecting it. It was because God *was* at work that he could pray with confidence.[1]

Read Ephesians 1:1–18

The love between the Father, Son, and Holy Spirit exploded into what we call a covenant of redemption. Before the triune God created, the Father set His affection on a people and chose them as His own. He gave His chosen ones to His Son, who accomplished their redemption with His own blood. The Holy Spirit applies the plan of the Father and the work of the Son to the hearts of the ones the Father gave the Son, and guarantees their share in God's eternal kingdom. From beginning to end it is seamless, sovereign grace.

Redemption is designed to praise the glorious grace of the glorious triune God (vv. 6, 12, 14). And indeed it does. A dead person being made alive to live in relationship with God and to reflect His glory is a mystery we cannot fully understand.

Although Christianity is not mysticism, there are profoundly mystical and spiritual dimensions that are inseparably bound up with the Christian faith. The message so focuses on the work of the Holy Spirit in our lives, and on the concept of supernatural and divine revelation, that we must be careful to rid our minds of the crass secularism that threatens to extinguish the biblical message in our day.[2]

Read this passage again—slowly. Paul's soaring doxology takes us *beyond* time and space to show us truths that should determine our life perspective and shape our prayers for ourselves and others. God's Word also brings His sovereignty *into* time and space to see our place in the redemption story.

> And he made from one man every nation of mankind to live on all the face of the earth, having determined allotted periods and the boundaries of their dwelling place, that they should seek God, in the hope that they might feel their way toward him and find him. Yet he is actually not far from each one of us, for "In him we live and move and have our being." (Acts 17:26–28)

God determined the exact time and place in history—the exact situations and relationships—to make known to us the grand mystery of His will to unite all things in Christ. What looks and feels like the collision of the parts of our lives is actually everything working together according to His will so that we—the ones He gave to Jesus—might stand as testimonies of His glorious grace. This knowledge prompts and propels us to reach up, grab our inheritance in Christ, and pull these riches down into our own lives and the lives of those for whom we pray. I rather think this is what Paul did. He was not stymied by his imprisonment because his life perspective was solidly based on his knowledge of God's sovereign love in Christ. So his praise transitioned into his petition.

Read Ephesians 1:15–16

The reason Paul dares to pray so boldly and persistently is the redemption planned, accomplished, and applied by the triune God. The faith of the saints in Ephesus, and their love for one another, are evidences of their redemption, so he gives thanks *for* them, not *to* them. He recognizes their faith and love for what they are—the work of God's grace. Paul prays without ceasing for this redemption to be made complete in them. This is a prayer for maturity in Christ.

It seems to me that children are an illustration of us all. They may be a little more obvious in their self-absorption, but not much. It takes little provocation for events and relationships to derail them—and us. But whenever we look at redeemed people—even those in desperate situations and those who are spiritually immature—we can thank God for His work of grace and ask Him to mature them.

Read Ephesians 1:17

The essence of maturity is knowing God, and this is Paul's petition. These are believers who already know God, but he is praying that the Holy Spirit will increase their knowledge. "Paul is not saying that Christians can expect to receive new revelations from God . . . he is saying that the Spirit works in Christians to help them understand the revelation (the Bible) God has already given."[3]

Read Ephesians 1:18–23

Paul continues his petition by asking God to open the eyes of believers' hearts. We can know facts intellectually, but we need the Holy Spirit to push truth into our hearts, or we will be like the Israelites who "refused to obey him . . . and in their hearts turned to Egypt" (Acts 7:39). When we are bent toward self, life seems muddled and we are functional life-takers. Paul's prayer counteracts this by asking God to open His people's hearts that they might know, deep in their souls, three great truths of salvation that will stabilize and sanctify them.

First, knowing the hope to which He has called us will anchor us. An eternal perspective of our hope in Christ inspires and encourages faithfulness.

> So when God desired to show more convincingly to the heirs of the promise the unchangeable character of his purpose, he guaranteed it with an oath, so that . . . we who have fled for refuge might have strong encouragement to hold fast to the hope set before us. We have this as a sure and steadfast anchor of the soul, a hope that enters into the inner place behind the curtain. (Heb. 6:17–19)

The anchored soul knows that nothing is random and nothing is wasted. The anchored soul draws near to God even when life seems fragmented and out of control. The anchored soul is a maturing soul.

Second, knowing that we are His inheritance assures us of His nearness.

Moses prayed, "O Lord, please let the Lord go in the midst of us, for it is a stiff-necked people, and pardon our iniquity and our sin, and take us for your inheritance" (Ex. 34:9). And He did. We are His treasured possession. We are the ones He adopts, redeems, forgives, and lavishes with His grace. We are the ones He loves even as He loves Jesus. We are the ones He keeps and sanctifies. We are the ones He will never leave. We are the ones He wants with Him to see His glory. Life begins to look grand and glorious rather than ragged and rudderless.

Third, knowing the greatness of the power in us instills confidence—not self-confidence but Christ-confidence.

Personalize Ephesians 1:19–20: "The same power that raised Jesus from the dead has been placed in me. He has given me his Spirit." We can live beyond our meager means. We can live large spiritually, and He piles up words and events to convince us so. He points to three proof-positive evidences of this power: the resurrection, ascension, and enthronement of Jesus.

> We are ready to admire chiefly the power of God in the visible world, but the soul of man is a far nobler creature than it. We justly admire the power of the Creator in the motion of the heavenly bodies; but the motion of souls towards God as their centre is far more glorious—the effects of the same power far more eminent and far more lasting.[4]

LIVING LARGE

Knowing Jesus is the unifying element of life. Too often I resort to puny prayers. I give the Lord a to-do list to solve the problems of those I'm praying for, and shamefully it is usually a list of behaviors *they* need to change that will make *my* life easier. But sometimes He delivers me from such smallness and I pray doxologically. I pray that the power that raised Jesus from the dead will enliven them to know Him more intimately. I pray to see the "motion of a soul toward God as his/her center." Paul prayed without ceasing, and so should we. Moving

110

a soul toward God is a lifelong process. But when the Lord begins to open the eyes of their hearts they begin to move from disorder to order, from immaturity to maturity. Their spirits begin to settle. The parts of their lives start to coalesce into one purpose—to praise God's glorious grace. And, as I pray thusly, *I* know Him better.

> The true woman thinks biblically. Regardless of the situation, she rests in God's sovereignty and prays that she will "grow in the grace and knowledge of our Lord and Savior Jesus Christ" (2 Peter 3:18).

How do we call on God in truth?

- Continually ask God to open the eyes of our hearts that we might know Him better.

LIFE-GIVING PRAYER

Movene Futch lives large in her small Georgia town. When she was asked to help organize a crisis pregnancy center in Forsyth, she prayed big and bold prayers. She prayed beyond the needs of opening the center. She prayed that God would open the way to teach sexual abstinence until marriage in the local schools. The committee made contacts, and occasionally was allowed to give a presentation in a school. The members continued to pray.

Ten years later the curriculum director of the local school system approached the committee about working together to lower teen pregnancy. Movene expressed eagerness to assist but explained that any program the committee taught would have to be from the perspective of abstinence until marriage. Remarkably, school officials said that this was what they wanted.

For ten more years the committee faithfully and prayerfully presented an excellent series to eighth-graders. During this time they strengthened their presentations and prayed that God would open the door to reach more grades. Then Movene received a call from the new school superintendent for the county, asking to meet with her. She, her church, and those who work with the pregnancy center prayed fervently. At the meeting the superintendent affirmed what they were teaching and requested that they expand. After twenty years of unceasing prayer, a team of Christian instructors, including Movene's pastor, now present a regular series to grades seven through twelve in all of the county schools. Movene says, "We prayed and God has given us the opportunity to share his plan that sex is to be within the bounds of marriage with over eighteen hundred students each year. To God be all praise and glory!"

Reflect and Pray

1. Reflect on Acts 17:26–28. How does knowing that God determined the time in history and the place on the planet where you would live change your perspective about the events and relationships in your life?
2. Use Paul's prayer in Ephesians 1:15–25 to write your prayer for yourself or someone else.
3. Reflect on Ephesians 1:19–23. What are your thoughts about having the same power that raised Jesus from the dead available to empower you to know and serve Him?

The LORD is near to all who call on him,
to all who call on him in truth.

Psalm 145:18

POWER

EPHESIANS 3:14−21

Reading Ephesians is exhilarating. Paul's exuberance about God's plan and purpose jumps from doxology to prayer to instruction and back again, yet with exquisite symmetry. It's as though Paul simply cannot get over the grace that transformed the persecutor of the church into the preacher of the church. He is enthralled with the wonder of our union with Christ and our union with one another.

What stands out about Ephesians is the awe with which it contemplates the mystery of the church. Ephesians describes the church as God's new humanity, a colony in which the Lord of history has established a foretaste of the renewed unity and dignity of the human race (1:10–14; 2:11–22; 3:6, 9–11; 4:1–6:9). The church is a community in which God's power to reconcile men and women to himself is experienced and then shared in transformed relationships.[1]

Paul's thrilling conclusion to his prayer in chapter one tells us that the Father "put all things under [Jesus'] feet and gave him as head over all things to the church, which is his body, the fullness of him who fills all in all" (22–23). Then Paul interrupts his prayer to teach us. The momentum builds until the words almost jump off the page in chapter three.

Read Ephesians 3:1–13

He almost starts to pray again—"For this reason"—but instead launches into an explanation of the mystery "that the Gentiles are fellow heirs, members of the same body, and partakers of the promise in Christ Jesus through the gospel" (3:6). The Old Testament hinted at this mystery but now, in Christ, it is revealed: The family of God is made up of people from every nation, tribe, people, and language (Revelation 7:9).

Then Paul returns to his prayer.

Read Ephesians 3:14–21

The reason for Paul's prayer is everything he has said since he started the letter. "An important principle of prayer emerges. The basis of Paul's prayer was his knowledge of God's purpose. . . . It is in Scripture that God has disclosed his will, and it is in prayer that we ask him to do it."[2]

Paul is dazzled with the spectacular singularity of the church and with the incredible intimacy of the church. He kneels—indicating God's majesty—yet he refers to God as the Father of a family, indicating God's nearness. He is mesmerized with the communion of the saints in heaven and on earth. Charles Spurgeon was too, and he used this text as a funeral sermon for a woman in his church.

> We cannot but sorrow this day, for the Lord has taken away a sister, a true servant of the church, a consecrated woman. . . . I have this day lost from my side one of the most faithful, fervent, and efficient of my helpers, and the church has lost one of her most useful members. Beloved, we need comfort, let us seek it where it may be found. I pray that we may view this source of grief, not with our natural, but with our spiritual eyes. . . . Take a steady look into the invisible, and the text, I think, sets before us something to gaze upon which may minister comfort to us. The saints in heaven, though apparently sundered from us, are in reality one with us; though death seems to have made breaches in the church of God, it is in fact perfect and entire; though the inhabitants of heaven and believers on earth might seem to be two orders of beings, yet in truth they are one family. . . . It is sweet to remember that all the saints in heaven and earth have the covenant promises secured to them . . . "I will be to them a God, and they shall be to Me a people."[3]

Then Paul prays big prayers for the church in Ephesus. In Ephesians 1 he prayed that they would have knowledge. Now he adds to that petition and asks for power. He divides his petition for power into two parts.

POWER TO CHANGE—VERSES 16–17

Our sanctification is the work of the triune God. Paul prays *to the Father*, that the Ephesians would be strengthened with power *through the Spirit,* in order that *Christ* would dwell in their hearts.

He is praying for Christians, because Christ already dwells in their hearts. But there are two Greek words for "dwell." *Paroikeo* refers to dwelling in a place as a stranger. The word used in verse 17 is *katoikeo,* which means to settle down in a place as a permanent residence. It's the difference between a hotel and a home. When I stay in a hotel I may not like the décor, but I don't waste time redecorating; however, Gene and I are continually repairing and redecorating our home. We once moved into an old house. We ripped out carpet, filled garbage bags with trash, and repainted. Soon it began to look like us. Now, our home is filled with almost fifty years of our shared life. Walk through our home and you know us better.

We need the power of the Holy Spirit to move the stuff in our hearts out to the trash pile and to give over more and more space to Jesus, so our hearts begin to look like Him. As He redecorates, mercy replaces indifference, graciousness replaces insensitivity, steadfast love replaces selfishness, faithfulness replaces fickleness, and forgiveness replaces bitterness. A hovel is transformed into a mansion. A life-taker is changed into a life-giver who has power to trash the idols in her heart and live for God's glory.

POWER TO LOVE—VERSES 17–19

Because of our union with Christ we have a new ability to love, but we need the power of the Holy Spirit for that love to grow. As Jesus occupies more space, the love roots go deeper. We are increasingly grounded. This refers to our love for one another.

The greatest commandment is that we "love the Lord your God with all your heart and with all your soul and with all your mind. . . . And a second is like it: You shall love your neighbor as yourself" (Matt. 22:37, 39). In Titus 2:3–5, older women are told to teach younger women how to love. Love can be commanded and it can be taught, because it is not just a feeling. Love is action. It is obedience. It is hard.

It takes enormous power to love others, and our Father provides this power. As we pray for the power of the Holy Spirit to love our husbands when they disappoint us, to love our children when they are rebellious, to love the people in our families and churches when they are difficult, there is an unexpected consequence. The unspeakable happens. We increasingly comprehend that which is incomprehensible and inexhaustible—God's love for us. This is something we do "with all the saints." There is an indivisible connection between our love for one another and our comprehension of God's love for us. According to John Stott, "It needs the whole people of God to understand the whole love of God."[4]

If we do not love others, our relationship with God is compromised and our understanding of His love is diminished. This does not mean that every relationship will always be two-sided. If the other person rejects our love, it is our opportunity to demonstrate the one-sidedness of the gospel, and when we do so our roots go deeper into God's love.

To know God's love beyond our capacity to know takes us to spiritual heights that are indescribably wonderful and to unity that is ineffably sublime. This is reminiscent of Jesus' prayer for our unity, and His provision of His glory to make that unity possible (John 17:20–23).

Paul keeps asking for more and more until he stuns us by asking that we be "filled with all the fullness of God." Boice explains, "I think Paul is praying that we will be filled and filled and filled and filled and filled—and so on forever, as God out of his infinite resources increasingly pours himself out into those sinful but now redeemed creatures he has rescued through the work of Christ."[5]

Doxology—Verses 20–21

Now Paul reaches for the sky. If we don't go where Paul takes us we miss the splendor of it all.

> Now to him who is able to do far more abundantly than all that we ask or think, according to the power at work within us, to him be glory in the church and in Christ Jesus throughout all generations, forever and ever. Amen. (20–21)

It's about Him—not us. Like Jesus (John 17:1), Paul prays for God to be glorified. God's glory and God's people are the first two themes in Jesus' prayer for us. The essence of Moses' prayer is "Show me your glory so I can love your people" (Exodus 33). Paul piles up words to urge us not to limit our prayers to what we can imagine ourselves or others doing and being. The resurrection power of Jesus is available to us so that we can glorify Him. We squander that resource by seeking personal comfort and pleasure for ourselves and others rather than His glory. To the degree that His glory is our passion, power increases—power to be changed into His likeness and to love His people. As we do so, His church is sanctified and unified and He is glorified.

The true woman is so heavenly minded that her prayers do earthly good.

How Do We Call on God in Truth?

- Ask for power to be filled with the fullness of God that He might be glorified in His church.

LIFE-GIVING PRAYER

Prayer is a grand mystery that is profoundly practical. I asked several true women to share practical prayer ideas. Here is a summary of what they told me.

- I had trouble keeping up with prayer requests until I started using index cards and a box with dividers. There is a divider marked "every" for daily requests. There are dividers for each day of the week and I use these for "categories" such as missionaries and church needs. Sometimes I write specific verses on the cards. I also write dates when I begin to pray and answers to prayer. Cards come and go as family, relationships, and needs change.
- Each Saturday I pray through portions of Psalm 119 to prepare my heart for worship.
- When someone asks me to pray for them I respond by saying, "I am asking God right now to remind me to pray for you." He is faithful to remind me, thus keeping me from making commitments I do not keep.
- On our grandchildren's birthdays I write a prayer for them, based on a specific Scripture, in my prayer journal.
- I love to sing through hymns that help me to praise God.
- Sometimes I use *Valley of Vision*, a collection of Puritan prayers. This is especially helpful when I am in a crisis and have difficulty focusing.

- I pray for people as I drive, especially if I am driving by their home.
- When someone shares a problem or concern I ask, "How can I pray for you?" If possible I pray with her immediately and then follow up later by telling her the specific Scripture I am praying.
- In the front of my prayer journal I have a prayer list for each day, then a section for journaling. I don't journal every day, but when I do I "listen" to the Lord first by reading His Word, then write the Scripture reference and date at the top of the page. My prayers and meditations flow out of what I read.
- Before bedtime I write things I'm thankful for from that day: a warm bed, my loving husband lying beside me, lunch with a friend, a finished project, a conversation that strengthened a relationship, the snow. I thank the Lord for these undeserved gifts. I started this to develop gratitude and fight a selfish heart. I've been surprised that my quality of sleep has improved!

Reflect and Pray

1. What are some things you need strength to change?
2. Who are people you need power to love? Why are they difficult for you to love?
3. How would you explain the connection between our love for others and our understanding of God's love for us?

The LORD *is near to all who call on him,*
to all who call on him in truth.

Psalm 145:18

11

LIFE

1 Samuel 1:1 — 2:10

The book of Judges concludes with these ominous words: "In those days there was no king in Israel. Everyone did what was right in his own eyes" (Judg. 21:25).

After the period of the judges comes a transition to a new social order under which God installs a king in Israel. This mega-moment in the redemption story hinges on Hannah, an obscure, barren woman. God often startles us by using the foolish to shame the wise, the weak to overcome the strong, and the obscure to shape the culture, "so that no human being might boast in the presence of God" (1 Cor. 1:29).

Hannah was a remarkable woman, but I suspect that never occurred to her. She was an ordinary Jewish woman who lived each day in the context of her relationships and circumstances, but I think the text shows a subtle distinction that set her apart. She didn't flaunt the distinction; it was simply there. She was a true woman. Her relationships show that she was a life-giver, and her prayers show why.

HANNAH'S RELATIONSHIPS

Read 1 Samuel 1:1–7

The first relationship is identified as Hannah's rival. Rivalries among women are usually relational, and they are usually ugly.

Hannah's infertility was a source of pain, and Peninnah was merciless. She taunted Hannah year after year, but there is no indication that Hannah retaliated. Hannah means "gracious woman," and indeed she was. She was also wise. She seems to have realized that this was a relationship she could not "fix," so she followed the wisdom of Proverbs: "Good sense makes one slow to anger, and it is his glory to overlook an offense" (19:11). Peninnah was a life-taker in that home; Hannah was a life-giver.

Perhaps the key to Hannah's quiet and gracious heart is seen in the twice-repeated phrase, "the LORD had closed her womb" (1 Sam. 1:5, 6). She humbly acknowledges and accepts God's sovereignty so the interminable irritation of her rival does not wear her down. She is sad but she is strong. Her pain matures her. She puts flesh on 1 Peter 5:6–7:

> Clothe yourselves, all of you, with humility toward one another, for "God opposes the proud but gives grace to the humble." Humble yourselves, therefore, under the mighty hand of God so that at the proper time he may exalt you, casting all your anxieties on him, because he cares for you.

Read 1 Samuel 1:8–9

Hannah's husband meant well but he lacked understanding. Hannah, however, did not criticize him. Perhaps she had heard the story of Sarah's solution to infertility.

> And Sarai said to Abram, "Behold now, the Lord has prevented me from bearing children. Go in to my servant; it may be that I shall obtain children by her." And Abram listened to the voice of Sarai. (Gen. 16:2)

Sarah lost her grip on God's sovereignty and trusted her own scheme. We run amuck when we think we have to fix everything. Things got dicey when Hagar became pregnant.

> And Sarai said to Abram, "May the wrong done to me be on you! I gave my servant to your embrace, and when she saw that she had conceived, she looked on me with contempt. May the Lord judge between you and me! But Abram said to Sarai, "Behold, your servant is in your power; do to her as you please." Then Sarai dealt harshly with her, and she fled from her. (Gen. 16:5–6)

This is the convoluted logic of a life-taker: "You did what I told you. I'm still unhappy. It's your fault!" Abraham threw up his hands and walked away from the situation. This scenario has been replayed through the ages, when a woman is a life-taker, and then she wonders why her husband is passive. Perhaps Hannah learned from Sarah's failure.

This moment in Sarah's life gives me great hope, because by God's grace she went on to become one of "the holy women who hoped in God" (1 Peter 3:4–6), and Abraham "believed against hope, that he should become the father of many nations, as he had been told. . . . He grew strong in his faith as he gave glory to God, fully convinced that God was able to do what he had promised" (Rom. 4:18, 20–21).

Hannah exemplifies 1 Peter 4:8: "Above all, keep loving one another earnestly, since love covers a multitude of sins." She listened to her husband's gentle rebuke and acted responsibly. She ate, went to the temple, and prayed.

Read 1 Samuel 1:10–18

Hannah's pastor, Eli the priest, falsely accused her. She could have caused an uproar in the church and community if she had broadcast this injustice, but she didn't. With her rival and her husband, Hannah overlooked the offense. But this situation needed a response—not just for Hannah, but for Eli.

Hannah dug deep into her soul and again submitted to the sovereignty of God. She spoke to Eli with respect and humility by referring to him as "my lord" and to herself as "your servant." Rather than project a syrupy, superficial spirituality, she eloquently explained the situation with dignity and clarity. Hannah did not back Eli into a verbal corner. He recovered quickly and blessed her. She helped him to be a better pastor. Hannah was a life-giver in the church.

Read 1 Samuel 1:19–28

The Lord answered Hannah's prayer, and when Samuel was weaned she fulfilled her vow to give him to the Lord to serve in the temple. In the Old Testament a woman could make a vow but her husband could nullify it (Num. 30:10–15). Hannah made a radical vow. Elkanah could have reasoned: "She was under a lot of stress. If she keeps this vow she'll be miserable and I'll never hear the end of it." But he affirmed her vow. Here is a husband whose heart trusted his wife (Prov. 31:11). Trust does not happen overnight. Trust accrues year after year as a woman is a life-giver in a myriad of relationships and circumstances.

> Hannah is portrayed as the most pious woman in the Old Testament. Here she is shown going up to the Lord's house; no other woman in the Old Testament is mentioned doing this. In addition, Hannah is the only woman shown making and fulfilling a vow to the Lord; she is also the only woman who is specifically said to pray. . . . Her prayer is also among the longest recorded in the Old Testament.[1]

Hannah is stunning, but if we stop here we reduce Scripture to an engaging story with a good moral. Hannah would be horrified if we ended her story with "What would Hannah do?" Her relationships are the backdrop of the drama, but her prayers tell the gospel story.

HANNAH'S PRAYERS

Re-read 1 Samuel 1:10–11

Hannah's petition shows that she was a recipient of sovereign grace. She addresses God as "LORD of hosts." This title is used in verse 3, but verse 11 is the first time in Scripture that it is used in prayer. God had made Himself known to her as LORD—Yahweh—His personal name of covenant faithfulness to His people. To this she adds the term "hosts."

> [This] has traditionally been understood as a military term meaning "hosts" or "armies." In this sense, the reference would seem to encompass the hosts of Israel, the cosmic hosts and the angelic hosts. The title would then be expressive of the Lord's sovereignty over all earthly and heavenly powers to use them to carry out his will against opposition.[2]

Hannah calls on God in truth. She brings together the two seemingly incompatible concepts of God's sovereign transcendence (hosts) and His nearness (LORD). Her intimacy with Him was not just emotional; it was also theological.

Three times Hannah identifies herself as the Lord's servant, underscoring her submission to His authority. The name of the Lord was her strong tower, and this righteous woman ran into Him for safety (Prov. 18:10).

Read 1 Samuel 2:1–10

Hannah's theologically rich prayer shows that she knew God's Word and His character. This is what shaped her life, relationships, and prayers.

Verses 1–2. Hannah's joy was ultimately in the Giver of the gift, not the gift. She was grateful for Samuel but he was not the source of her joy. This is what Jesus referred to in John 17:13:

"These things I speak in the world, that they may have *my joy* fulfilled in themselves." Hannah's prayer of praise would have been the same if she had not been given a baby. I think this is the joy that sustained her year after year as she struggled with infertility.

The personal pronouns show the intimacy of her relationship with the Lord, and her switch to the plural—"no rock like *our* God"—shows that she understood her place in the covenant community. She saw herself united with the company of the redeemed throughout the ages.

The images she uses for God indicate her knowledge of the Torah. As she rejoiced in His holiness perhaps she remembered Leviticus 11:45: "For I am the Lord who brought you up out of the land of Egypt to be your God. You shall therefore be holy, for I am holy."

She may have learned of His uniqueness—"there is no one besides you"—from Moses' song: "Who is like you, O LORD, among the gods? Who is like you, majestic in holiness, awesome in glorious deeds, doing wonders?" (Ex. 15:11).

And did she remember Moses' prayer, "Show me your glory," and God's instruction, "Stand on the rock," and his promise, "I will put you in a cleft of the rock" (Ex. 33:21–22)? There is no question that the glorious goodness God showed to Moses—His mercy, graciousness, slowness to anger, steadfast love, faithfulness, and forgiveness (Ex. 34:6–7)—was reflected by Hannah to those around her.

Verses 3–8. She rejoices in the sovereignty of God and not in her circumstances. There is no reason for boasting or despair because He is the reverser of circumstances.

Israelite faith is at its core teleological [the doctrine that final causes exist; there is purpose and design]. It insists that Yahweh will ultimately straighten out every crookedness and judge every sin. While consistently taking a pessimistic view of the human condition, it nevertheless insists that the present order must be viewed with the awareness that God will ultimately transform the prevailing conditions. Though human beings are capable of much good, the corruptions of human nature assure that much evil will be done; however, the injustices of this present age are not permanent. In his day Yahweh will sweep them aside and bring about an era when justice will prevail.[3]

Or, as Mr. Beaver says:

> Wrong will be right, when Aslan comes in sight,
> As the sound of his roar, sorrows will be no more,
> When he bares his teeth, winter meets its death,
> And when he shakes his mane, we shall have spring again.[4]

Verses 9–10. Hannah's astonishing conclusion of joyful hope looks beyond David, whom Samuel would anoint, to the kingdom of Christ. Hannah points us to Jesus! She was not intoxicated with wine but with the majesty of the Messiah. Hannah was a life-giver because of Jesus.

The true woman's life points to Jesus the Giver of life.

HANNAH'S LEGACY

Whether a woman is a life-giver or a life-taker her legacy is, to some degree, passed on to the next generation. Hannah's life-giving legacy traveled through the years to a teenage girl in Nazareth. When young Mary is told that her virgin womb will carry the Life of the world, she identifies herself as a servant: "Behold, I am the servant of the Lord; let it be to me according to your word" (Luke 1:38). Had she been discipled with the story of Hannah? I think so because her prayer of praise, her Magnificat (Luke 1:46–55), is strikingly similar to Hannah's prayer.

We don't know what happened to Peninnah but we do know that God is the Redeemer of our failures and the Reverser of our legacies. Even if a woman does not become a life-giver until late in life, God's grace can raise her from the dust, lift her legacy from the ash heap, make her sit with princesses, and inherit a seat of honor (1 Sam. 2:8).

How do we call on God in truth?
• Humbly submitting to His sovereignty.

LIFE-GIVING PRAYER

Prayers travel a long way. They are not limited by a lifespan. During a question-and-answer session at a conference, a woman asked: "How can I give a legacy to my grandchildren? My daughter and her husband are not Christians and they threaten not to let me see the children if I mention anything about the Lord or church." I said the only reasonable thing to say in such a situation, "Let's pray." We did, and then I heard myself suggesting something I do not remember thinking previously. "I encourage you to write your prayers for your grandchildren. Some day perhaps they, or their children, will see your prayer journal and know they were prayed for."

Then we were surprised when the man working the sound system told us his story. "I became a Christian a few years ago and thought I was the first Christian in my family. Later I was given a journal that belonged to my great-grandmother, whom I never met. She prayed for the generations to come in her family. I am an answer to her prayers. I am not a first-generation Christian. I have a legacy."

Reflect and Pray

1. What did you learn from Hannah's responses to her relationships? What characteristics of a life-giver do you see in her?
2. What did you learn from Hannah's prayers? How did she call on God in truth?
3. Read Mary's Magnificat in Luke 1:46–55 and list similarities to Hannah's prayer in 1 Samuel 2:1–10.

The LORD is near to all who call on him,

to all who call on him in truth.

Psalm 145:18

12

KINGDOM

MATTHEW 6:9—13

When we began this prayer pilgrimage, I did not know why my outline started with John 17 and ended with the Lord's Prayer. It just seemed a good idea to begin and end with Jesus! I thought of reversing the order, but now I'm glad I didn't. John 17 tells us that we belong to Jesus because the Father gave us to Him, that Jesus sends us into the world, and that He prays for us as we go. Matthew 6 teaches us how to pray as we live in the kingdom of darkness while extending the kingdom of light and waiting for the kingdom of glory. Think about it—that is the focus of every prayer we have studied. As John MacArthur says, "The focus of biblical praying is the glory of God and the extension of his kingdom."[1]

THE KINGDOM OF GOD

I will extol you, my God and King . . . Your kingdom is an everlasting kingdom, and your dominion endures through-out all generations. (Ps.145:1, 13)

God made everything; it is His. As Owner and King He *rules* and *reigns*. Throughout the Old Testament He exerted His rule primarily through Israel. When Jesus came, He inaugurated God's worldwide rule in the hearts of His people from every nation, and there is more to come when Jesus returns and we see the fullness of His glory.

When Jesus started His ministry He "began to preach, saying, 'Repent, for the kingdom of heaven is at hand'" (Matt. 4:17). He preached the Sermon on the Mount, which teaches the ethics of God's kingdom. One section in this masterful sermon teaches us how to pray. Prayer is a privilege and responsibility of kingdom people. In John 17 Jesus prays for His church. In this prayer He teaches His church how to pray for each other and for the world. It is a Great Commission prayer. In *Making Kingdom Disciples*, Charles Dunahoo says, "Christ is the King and head of the church, her Lord and master, but he is also the Lord of the universe. As Christians, belonging to Christ's church, move out into the broader area of the kingdom as salt and light, God intends that their lives make an impact in every area of life."[2]

The kingdom idea is spectacular. Praying kingdom prayers lifts us above the fray and reminds us whose we are and the glorious inheritance we have in Him. Sometimes it looks and feels as if the world is winning, but Psalm 2 sets the record straight:

> The kings of the earth set themselves,
> and the rulers take counsel together,
> against the LORD and against his anointed . . .
>
> He who sits in the heavens laughs;
> . . . .
> Then he will speak to them in his wrath,
> . . . . saying,

"As for me, I have set my King
   on Zion, my holy hill."

I will tell of the decree;
The LORD said to me, "You are my Son;
   today I have begotten you.
Ask of me, and I will make the nations your heritage,
   and the ends of the earth your possession."
. . . .

Now therefore, O kings, be wise
. . . .
Serve the LORD with fear,
   and rejoice with trembling.
. . . .
Blessed are all who take refuge in him. (Ps. 2:2, 4–8, 10–12)

THE LORD'S PRAYER

Some suggest that John 17 should be called the Lord's Prayer and this should be called the disciples' prayer. I think they both should be called the Lord's Prayer because no one but our Savior could have prayed John 17 and no one but Jesus could teach us to pray. Consider what others have said about this prayer:

D. Martyn Lloyd-Jones:

> The amazing and extraordinary thing about it is that it really covers everything in principle. There is a sense in which you can never add to the Lord's Prayer; nothing is left out. . . . Take that great prayer of our Lord's which is recorded in John 17. . . .

If you analyse it in terms of principles, you will find that it can be reduced to the principles of this model prayer.[3]

Thomas Houston:

> In every expression, petition, and argument of this prayer, we see Jesus: He and the Father are one. He has a "Name" given him which is above every name. . . . His "kingdom" ruleth over all. He is the "living bread." . . . He had power on earth to "forgive sins." He is able to succor them that are "tempted,". . . The Kingdom, power, and glory pertain unto him. . . . Well did Tertullian term the Lord's Prayer "the Gospel abbreviated." The more clearly we understand the Gospel of the grace of God, "the Gospel of the glory of Christ," the more shall we love this wonderful prayer.[4]

This is a model for prayer. We might think of it as an outline. Jesus gives us the principles or categories and we are to personalize it and fill in the details. It is a perfect outline; no category is missing.

Read Matthew 6:9–13

The preface of the Lord's Prayer, which is, *Our Father which art in heaven*, teacheth us to draw near to God with all holy reverence and confidence, as children to a father, able and ready to help us; and that we should pray with and for others. (Westminster Shorter Catechism Q. 100)

In John 17 Jesus looked up to heaven and said, "Father . . ." We learned in chapter 3 that this is the unique name of God that

Jesus reveals to us. This familial relationship with the King was a new concept. He uses the plural "our," indicating that through Him we have been adopted into God's family. We belong to Jesus and we belong to each other. I'm not sure we can imagine the shock and awe the disciples experienced when they heard that they were to approach the Holy of Holies with such intimacy. If we ponder this, we too will be wonder-struck.

By His grace He is our Father. In gratitude for our redemption we should honor and submit to Him. When our children are difficult, dismissive, or disrespectful, it should prompt us to examine our own hearts and lives before our Father.

Jesus immediately adds "in heaven" to remind us that our Father is the King.

> What a blessed balance this gives to the previous phrase. If that tells us of God's goodness and grace, this speaks of his greatness and majesty. If that teaches us of the nearness and dearness of his relationship to us, this announces his infinite elevation above us. If the words "Our Father" inspire confidence and love, then the words "which art in heaven" should fill us with humility and awe. These are the two things that should ever occupy our minds and engage our hearts: the first without the second tends toward unholy familiarity; the second without the first produces coldness and dread.[5]

There are six petitions. The first three refer to God and the last three to our concerns. We see this same pattern in the Ten Commandments and in John 17.

> In the first petition, which is, *Hallowed be thy name*, we pray that God would enable us, and others, to glorify him in all that whereby he maketh himself known; and that he

would dispose all things to his own glory. (Westminster Shorter Catechism Q. 101)

Hallowed means set apart for a sacred use, treated as holy. The name of God stands for all that He has revealed to us about Himself. In John 17 Jesus' first petition was for God's glory.

God's glory should be the goal of our lives and of every petition. We bear His name. Our thoughts, words, and actions hallow or desecrate that precious name. The world and our sinful hearts desensitize us. We need His presence and His power to honor His name, to long for the whole world to do so, and to look forward to that time when it will be so.

> In the second petition, which is, *Thy kingdom come*, we pray that Satan's kingdom may be destroyed; and that the kingdom of grace may be advanced, ourselves and others brought into it, and kept in it, and that the kingdom of glory may be hastened. (Westminster Shorter Catechism Q. 102)

These petitions follow a logical order. We pray for His name to be hallowed because it is not. There is another kingdom that opposes God's rule and reign, so our prayer moves on to pray for God's kingdom to come. This is personal, global, and cosmic— rule in my heart, in the hearts of your people, in whatever place you have put each of us to live out your kingdom realities, and ultimately throughout the world when Christ returns.

> In the third petition, which is, *Thy will be done in earth, as it is in heaven*, we pray that God, by his grace, would make us able and willing to know, obey, and submit to his will in all things, as the angels do in heaven. (Westminster Shorter Catechism Q. 103)

The issue here is governance—God's will or my will. In *A Praying Life*, Paul E. Miller says, "Self-will and prayer are both ways of getting things done. At the center of self-will is me, carving a world in my image, but at the center of prayer is God, carving me in his Son's image."[6]

> The true woman is glad she cannot change herself or others, because she does not trust her own will. She knows that God is the changer of hearts and that His will is good.

The remaining requests for our needs are ultimately about glorifying God and extending His kingdom. The pronouns are plural, which indicates that we are to make these requests also for the family of God.

> In the fourth petition, which is, *Give us this day our daily bread*, we pray that of God's free gift we may receive a competent portion of the good things of this life, and enjoy his blessing with them. (Westminster Shorter Catechism Q. 104)

Jesus tells us to pray for our physical needs. A kingdom person knows that "The earth is the LORD's and the fullness thereof, the world and those who dwell therein" (Ps. 24:1), so it is logical to ask Him for the necessities of life. It all belongs to our Father, and we are stewards of the things He entrusts to us. Asking reminds us of our dependence and engenders gratitude for His provisions. His children are compassionate, so we ask Him to provide for others.

In the fifth petition, which is, *And forgive us our debts, as we forgive our debtors,* we pray that God, for Christ's sake, would freely pardon all our sins; which we are the rather encouraged to ask, because by his grace we are enabled from the heart to forgive others. (Westminster Shorter Catechism Q. 105)

We are to pray about our relationships with others. Unity in relationships hinges on forgiveness. This petition does not ask for forgiveness *because* we forgive others. The only way of forgiveness is through the substitutionary atonement of Jesus, but the forgiven become forgivers. Grace so transforms their hearts that they reflect the forgiving heart of their Savior even to those who hurt them. Forgiveness is compelling evidence of our citizenship: "The glory that you have given me I have given to them, that they may be one . . . so that the world may know that you sent me and loved them even as you love me" (John 17:22–23).

In the sixth petition, which is, *And lead us not into temptation, but deliver us from evil,* we pray that God would either keep us from being tempted to sin, or support and deliver us when we are tempted. (Westminster Shorter Catechism Q. 106)

We are to pray about our relationship with God. We ask our Father for the same thing our Savior prayed for us: "Keep them from the evil one . . . sanctify them in the truth" (John 17:15, 17).

The conclusion of the Lord's Prayer, which is, *For thine is the kingdom, and the power, and the glory, forever. Amen,* teacheth us to take our encouragement in prayer from God only, and in our prayers to praise him, ascribing kingdom, power, and glory to him; and, in testimony of our desire, and assurance to be heard, we say, Amen. (Westminster Shorter Catechism Q. 107)

This doxology is the basis and goal of every petition. Prayer should always move us forward and upward to His rule and reign in the new heaven and the new earth. "Amen" expresses our assurance that it will be so.

> The perfections of this prayer as a whole and the wondrous fullness of each clause and word in it are not perceived by a rapid and careless glance, but become apparent only by a reverent pondering. . . . In this prayer our Lord gives us the quintessence of true prayer.[7]

How do we call on God in truth?

• By praying as He taught us to pray.

The true woman knows that God is near and that she draws nearer to Him when she prays as He taught her to pray.

LIFE-GIVING PRAYER

On my Mother's ninetieth birthday she wanted to give a gift to her children, grandchildren, and great-grandchildren, so we made a "Grandma Mac's Recipes and Stories" booklet for each one. In it, she wrote a letter to us. Here are some excerpts from her letter:

> Our Lord has blessed me with a big family and I'm so thankful to him for you. I pray for each of you by name and for the generations to come. . . .
>   I didn't get to see my Grandma Barnes very often (her name was Kathryn, but Grandpa called her Cassie) but I

remember she prayed for us. She was a sweet, quiet little lady, and a godly one. She always said something that stayed with me. . . . I will say to you what she asked us: "Will I see you in heaven?" I pray so.

I love each of you, Grandma Mac. (Mary Kathryn McLaurin)

Reflect and Pray

1. Read Matthew 6:5–8. What does Jesus warn against?
   - By contrast, what is the focus in verses 9–13?
2. How do the last three petitions glorify God and extend His kingdom?
3. Take your prayer concerns and place each one under one of the principles in this prayer.

PRAYERS FROM SCRIPTURE

It is, therefore, by the benefit of prayer that we reach those riches which are laid up for us with the Heavenly Father.
—John Calvin, *Institutes of the Christian Religion*

These prayers are based on passages in this study. You may want to use them to pray for others, or adapt them to pray for yourself. If you are married, adapt them to pray for your husband and yourself.

Father, give me wisdom to faithfully declare Your mighty acts to _____. Please be near them and empower them to call on You in truth, to glorify You in all things, and to fulfill Your calling for them. Psalm 145:4, 18; Ephesians 1; John 17:4

Holy Father, keep _____ by the power of Your name. Keep them from all evil. Keep their going out and their coming in. John 17:11; Psalm 121

Strong Father, by Your grace, cause _____ to run away from sin and to run into the strong tower of Your name. May they always seek safety in You. Proverbs 18:10

Righteous Father, sanctify _____ by the power of Your Word. Turn their hearts to Your Word. Turn them away from worthless things and turn them to the Worthy One. John 17:17; Psalm 119:36–37

Glorious Father, show _____ the goodness of Your character—Your mercy, graciousness, slowness to anger, steadfast love and faithfulness, and forgiveness. May Your goodness grow in their hearts so that there might be unity in their relationships that will glorify You and be a witness of Your love. Exodus 34:6–7; John 17:20–23

Holy Father, show _____ Your ways that they may know You. Do awesome things with them. Transform them by the power of Your gospel from glory to glory. Exodus 33:13; Exodus 34:10; 2 Corinthians 3:18

Merciful Father, teach _____ truth and wisdom in their secret hearts. Create in them a clean heart. Open their lips to declare Your praise. May their passion be Your glory and Your people. Psalm 51

Forgiving Father, give _____ a deeper and deeper understanding of the magnitude of the sin debt Jesus paid for them. May gratitude for Your forgiveness drive them to have mercy on those who hurt them and to forgive from the heart. Matthew 18:32–35

Loving Father, give _____ a holy resolve to humble themselves before You, to seek You with all their hearts, to turn from their wicked ways, and to seek first Your kingdom and Your righteousness. 2 Chronicles 7:14; Matthew 6:33

Faithful Father, thank You that Your eyes and Your heart are always on the ones You gave to Jesus. May the eyes and hearts of _____ always be on You. 2 Chronicles 7:15–17; 20:12

Lord God of Abraham, Isaac, and Jacob, when enemies come against _____ may they pray, "We do not know what to do but our eyes are on You." Give them quietness and trust that they may stand firm and remember that the battle is Yours. May they go forward in faith and gather the blessings You have for those who trust and obey Your Word. 2 Chronicles 20; Isaiah 30:15

Gracious Father, I pray that _____ will trust in You with all their hearts and never lean on their own understanding. Turn their hearts to acknowledge Your sovereignty in every situation and relationship and to walk in Your straight paths. Proverbs 3:5–6

Praise to You Father, Son, and Holy Spirit. I thank You for _____ and pray that You will give them a spirit of wisdom and insight that they might know You more and more. Open the eyes of their hearts that they might know the hope to which You have called them and the power of the resurrected Christ working in them to live for Your glory. Ephesians 1:18–23

I bow before You Father and ask that according to the riches of Your glory You will give _____ strength through Your Spirit in their inner being so that Christ might increasingly dwell in their hearts through faith. May Jesus occupy more and more space in their hearts. May they decrease and Jesus increase. Ephesians 3:14–17; John 3:30

Father of love, may _____ be rooted and grounded in love. Give them strength to understand beyond their capacity the breadth and length and height and depth of Your love for them. May they be compelled by that love to love others as You love them. Ephesians 3:17–19

Lord God of heaven and earth, fill _____ with all the fullness of Yourself. Do more in them than I can ask or think, according to Your power at work within them, and all for Your glory in the church and in Christ Jesus throughout all generations. Ephesians 3:19–21

Lord Almighty, I pray that _____ will rejoice and rest in Your sovereignty over all things and that You will guard their feet and give them strength to do Your will. 1 Samuel 1:11; 2:9–10

Our Father in heaven, give _____ grace today to honor Your name and do Your will on earth as it is done in heaven. I pray that each day they will grow in the grace and knowledge of Jesus. Matthew 6:9–10; 2 Peter 3:18

Father, provide for _____ according to Your will. May they be so grateful for forgiveness in Christ that they will be forgivers. Lead them away from temptation and deliver them from evil. Matthew 6:11–13

Father, may _____ live in a way that their lives are worthy of the gospel. I pray that Your Spirit will produce the gospel fruit of love, joy, peace, patience, kindness, goodness, faithfulness, gentleness, and self-control in them. In the name and for the glory of Jesus. Philippians 1:21; Galatians 5:22–23

NOTES

Introduction

1. For more information on Titus 2 discipleship, see *Women's Ministry Training and Resource Guide*, available from the PCA Bookstore, 1–800–283–1357, or www.cepbookstore.com.

2. Susan Hunt, *The True Woman* (Wheaton, Ill.: Crossway Books, 1997), 22.

Chapter One: Redeemed

1. Westminster Shorter Catechism Q. 6 (Atlanta: PCA Committee for Christian Education & Publications, 1990), 4.

2. Wayne Grudem, *Evangelical Feminism & Biblical Truth* (Sisters, Ore.: Multnomah Publishers, 2004), 45–48.

3. Susan Hunt, *By Design* (Wheaton, Ill.: Crossway Books, 1994), 109. The story is from a newsletter of First Presbyterian Church, Columbia, S.C.

Chapter Two: Glorifiy

1. Arthur W. Pink, *Exposition of the Gospel of John, Vol. 3* (Grand Rapids: Zondervan Publishing House, 1945), 89.

2. Ibid., 90.

3. James Montgomery Boice, *The Gospel of John, Vol. 4, Peace in Storm* (Grand Rapids: Baker Books, 1985, 1999), 1247.

4. Pink, *Exposition of the Gospel of John, Vol. 3*, 93.

5. Boice, *The Gospel of John, Vol. 4*, 1248.

6. R. Laird Harris, Gleason L. Archer Jr., and Bruce K. Waltke, *Theological Wordbook of the Old Testament, Vol. 1* (Chicago: Moody Press, 1980), 427.

7. Charles Haddon Spurgeon, *The Treasury of the Bible, New Testament, Vol. 2* (Grand Rapids: Zondervan Publishing House, 1962), 599.

8. Boice, *The Gospel of John, Vol. 4*, 1250.

9. Susan Olasky, "In the Thick of It," *World* magazine, vol. 25, no. 21 (2010): 65.

Chapter Three: Sanctify

1. Boice, *The Gospel of John, Vol. 4*, 1272.

2. Ibid., 1290.

3. D. Martyn Lloyd-Jones, *Sanctified Through the Truth: The Assurance of Our Salvation* (Westchester, Ill.: Crossway Books, 1989), 8.

4. Westminster Shorter Catechism, Q. 35.

5. *English Standard Version Study Bible* (Wheaton, Ill.: Crossway Bibles, 2008), 2059.

6. Pink, *Exposition of the Gospel of John, Vol. 3*, 322–23.

7. James Montgomery Boice, *Psalms Vol. 3* (Grand Rapids: Baker Books, 1998), 1074–75.

Chapter Four: Unify

1. Spurgeon, *The Treasury of the Bible, New Testament, Vol. 2*, 611.

2. Boice, *The Gospel of John, Vol. 4*, 1333.

3. Spurgeon, *The Treasury of the Bible, New Testament, Vol. 2*, 618.

4. Sharon Betters' *Treasures of Encouragement* and *Treasures in Darkness* are testimonies of God's grace to her.

Chapter Five: Nearness

1. S. G. DeGraff, *Promise and Deliverance, Vol. 1* (St. Catharines, Ontario, Canada: Paideia Press, 1971), 255–56.

2. Arthur W. Pink, *Gleanings in Exodus* (Chicago: Moody Press, 1971), 346–47.

3. Ibid, 355.

Chapter Six: Forgiven

1. Alexander Maclaren, *Expositions of Holy Scripture, Genesis, Exodus, Leviticus and Numbers* (Charleston, S.C.: BiblioBazaar, 2006), 483.

2. Ibid.

3. Ibid.

4. Paul David Tripp, *Whiter Than Snow* (Wheaton, Ill.: Crossway Books, 2008), 142.

5. John Calvin, *Calvin's Commentaries, Psalms Vol. 2* (Grand Rapids: Zondervan Publishing, reprinted 1948, 1955, 1963), 298.

6. James Montgomery Boice, *An Expositional Commentary, Psalms, Vol. 2, Psalms 42–106* (Grand Rapids: Baker Books, 1996), 434.

7. Tripp, *Whiter Than Snow*, 71–72

Chapter Seven: Forgiving

1. Joseph V. Novenson, "Forgiveness, A Mark of a Healthy Church," *Tabletalk* 12 (2006), 54–55.

Chapter Eight: Help

1. James Montgomery Boice, *Ephesians: An Expositional Commentary* (Grand Rapids: Baker Book, 1998), 259.

2. C. H. Spurgeon, *The Treasury of the Bible: Old Testament, Vol. 2, 1 Chronicles to Psalm CXI* (Grand Rapids: Zondervan, 1962), 74.

3. Stanley D. Gale, *The Prayer of Jehoshaphat* (Phillipsburg, N.J., P&R Publishing, 2007), 122.

4. Spurgeon, *The Treasury of the Bible: Old Testament, Vol. 2*, 76–77.

5. R. Laird Harris, Gleason L. Archer Jr., Bruce K. Waltke, *Theological Wordbook of the Old Testament, Vol. 2* (Chicago: Moody Press, 1980), 953.

6. Harris et al, *Theological Wordbook of the Old Testament, Vol. 1*, 101.

Chapter Nine: Knowledge

1. Boice, *Ephesians* (Grand Rapids: Baker Books, 1997), 33–34.

2. R. C. Sproul, *The Purpose of God: An Exposition of Ephesians* (Fearn, Scotland: Christian Focus Publications, 1994), 37.

3. Ibid., 38.

4. John M'Laurin, *Precious Seed: Discourses by Scottish Worthies*, sermon titled "Glorying in the Cross of Christ" (Birmingham, Ala.: Solid Ground Christian Books, 2007, reprinted from 1877 edition by John Grieg & Son, Edinburgh), 18.

Chapter Ten: Power

1. *Spirit of the Reformation Study Bible* (Grand Rapids: Zondervan, 2003), 1903.

2. John R. W. Stott, *The Message of Ephesians* (Downers Grove, Ill.: InterVarsity Press, 1979), 132.

3. C. H. Spurgeon, *The Treasury of the New Testament, Vol. 3* (Grand Rapids: Zondervan Publishing House, 1962), 412.

4. Quoted in D. A. Carson, *A Call to Spiritual Reformation* (Grand Rapids: Baker Academic, 1992), 198.

5. Boice, *Ephesians*, 112.

Chapter Eleven: Life

1. Robert D. Bergen, *The New American Commentary: An Exegetical and Theological Exposition of Holy Scripture: Vol. 7, 1, 2 Samuel* (Broadman & Holman Publishers, 1996), 67.

2. *Spirit of the Reformation Study Bible*, 394.

3. Bergen, *1, 2 Samuel*, 63.

4. C. S. Lewis, *The Lion, the Witch and the Wardrobe* (Harper Trophy, A Division of HarperCollins Publishers, 1950), 85.

Chapter Twelve: Kingdom

1. John MacArthur, *Elements of True Prayer* (Panorama City, Calif.: Word of Grace Communications, 1988), 62.

2. Charles H. Dunahoo, *Making Kingdom Disciples* (Phillipsburg, N.J.: P&R Publishing, 2005), 47.

3. D. Martyn Lloyd-Jones, *Studies in the Sermon on the Mount* (Grand Rapids: Wm. B. Eerdmans Publishing), 48–49.

4. Quoted in A. W. Pink, *The Beatitudes and the Lord's Prayer* (Grand Rapids: Baker Book House, 1979), 75–76.

5. Ibid, 80–81.

6. Paul E. Miller, *A Praying Life* (NavPress, 2009), 160–61.

7. Pink, *The Beatitudes and the Lord's Prayer*, 129–30.